Part Three: Putting Work in Its Proper Perspective!

Applying the Pentathlon: A Manual for Growth

An examination of your own struggles with balancing competing time demands.
A close look at a biblical model for planning called the Pentathlon.
How to find principles for godly living from the Bible and evaluate your own strengths and weaknesses in applying God's Word.
Setting goals in each of the five areas of the Pentathlon.
Developing a support system of people to encourage you in your growth.
A checklist you create will help measure your progress, and examine habits you want to cultivate or need to eliminate. You'll also evaluate what you've learned from this book.

HOW TO BALANCE

COMPETING

TIME

KEEPING THE FIVE MOST
IMPORTANT AREAS
OF YOUR LIFE
IN PERSPECTIVE

DEMANDS

DOUG SHERMAN & WILLIAM HENDRICKS

NAVPRESS
A MINISTRY OF THE NAVIGATORS
P.O. BOX 6000, COLORADO SPRINGS, COLORADO 80934

The Navigators is an international Christian organization. Jesus Christ gave His followers the Great Commission to go and make disciples (Matthew 28:19). The aim of The Navigators is to help fulfill that commission by multiplying laborers for Christ in every nation.

NavPress is the publishing ministry of The Navigators. NavPress publications are tools to help Christians grow. Although publications alone cannot make disciples or change lives, they can help believers learn biblical discipleship, and apply what they learn to their lives and ministries.

© 1989 by Doug Sherman and William Hendricks
All rights reserved, including translation
Library of Congress Catalog Card Number:
    89-61722
ISBN 08910-92277

Second printing, 1990

Scripture quotations in this publication are from the *New American Standard Bible* (NASB), © The Lockman Foundation 1960, 1962, 1963, 1968, 1971, 1972, 1973, 1975, 1977. Another version used is the *Holy Bible: New International Version* (NIV). Copyright © 1973, 1978, 1984, International Bible Society. Used by permission of Zondervan Bible Publishers.

NOTE: Throughout this book, where either the masculine or feminine pronouns are used, they should be understood as indicating both genders, unless the context implies otherwise.

Printed in the United States of America

Doug Sherman is the founder and president of Career Impact Ministries (CIM), a Christian organization that helps business and professional people integrate their faith into their careers.

After graduating from the Air Force Academy with a B.S. in engineering management, Doug served as an instructor in the Advanced Jet Training Program, a position he held until he left the Air Force to attend Dallas Theological Seminary, where he received a Th.M.

Doug and his wife, Jan, live in Woodbridge, Virginia, and have three children.

William Hendricks is a writer and consultant in communication development. He received a B.A. in English literature from Harvard University, an M.S. in mass communications from Boston University, and an M.A. from Dallas Theological Seminary. He is the former vice president of CIM.

Bill lives in Dallas, Texas, with his wife, Nancy, and their two daughters.

Other books by Doug Sherman and William Hendricks:

YOUR WORK MATTERS TO GOD (NavPress, 1988)

HOW TO SUCCEED WHERE IT REALLY COUNTS
(NavPress, 1989)

KEEPING YOUR ETHICAL EDGE SHARP
(NavPress, 1990)

ACKNOWLEDGMENTS

So many people have helped us in getting this book together, over so many years, that we'll probably never be able to acknowledge fully everyone's contribution. Still, we deeply appreciate the involvement of John Maisel, Ray Blunt, Butch McCaslin, Rick Nutter, Frank and Cathy Tanana, Bill McKenzie, Bill Robertson, Bill Anderson, Ed Johnson, Rex Sanders, Mike Middleton, Norm Miller, Jim Coté, Howard Hendricks, Wayne Hey, Bob Buford, Fred Smith Jr., and Jean Taft.

Another group that deserves special thanks for their wisdom, their faith in us, and their patience is John Eames, Bruce Nygren, Volney James, Steve Eames, and the entire NavPress team.

We also especially value the assistance of our irreplaceable "word processor," Karolynn Simmons.

And of course the "executive committee" of all these contributors, especially when it comes to balancing competing time demands, is made up of our wives and families: Jan, Jason, Matthew, and Jennifer Sherman, and Nancy, Brittany, and Kristin Hendricks. Some would say that apart from them we could have never fully appreciated the need for a book like this!

Doug Sherman
William Hendricks

Our friends laughed when we told them we were going to write a book called *How to Balance Competing Time Demands*. "You?" they asked incredulously. "That's a joke! When are *you* going to find time to do that? You're so swamped, you're the *last* people who should be writing on that subject!"

Well, we plead guilty to being busy. And if you're looking for someone to tell you how to completely avoid the avalanche of responsibilities that come with a job, a family, and just being alive, then we're probably not your boys.

On the other hand, if (like us) you want to face the normal challenges of life head on— if you don't want to run away from pressures, yet you also don't want to be overwhelmed by crushing demands on your time—then this book was written for you.

It's for the busy father who's trying to juggle a host of competing assignments and feels he's not doing too well in any of them. It's for the working mother who is torn between work and family, and knows that superwoman is only fiction from some Hollywood script-writer's imagination. It's for the single parent whose life boils down to her children and her work—and not a lot else. It's for the single person whose life is getting sucked into the black hole of an all-consuming career.

This book is for anyone who feels that life as it was intended to be lived has to be more than one giant deadline. It's not that we expect things to be easy or that we want to sail through life with abandon. But the frenetic busyness that passes for normalcy can't be right, either.

Is there an alternative? We believe there is—and you can read about it in the pages that follow.

AN ADDED BONUS

We've added something extra to this book to make it as useful as possible—a study guide that will help you apply the concepts presented to your life. We've included this material because we know how easy it is just to read a book and then put it on the shelf where it will accomplish nothing!

Instead, we really want to promote *life change*. We want to help you get control of your time and every area of your life, and that takes more than new ideas. It takes some practical guidelines and exercises for getting started.

So to get the most from this book, read it in conjunction with the material at the back called "Applying the Pentathlon: A Manual for Growth." Better yet, go through this material with a group of friends who are struggling with the same issue. You'll be amazed at how helpful the group dynamics will be to everyone's progress.

DUAL AUTHORSHIP

When you start reading, you'll notice that we use the first person singular: "I," "me," "my," etc. The voice you hear is Doug's, but this book has two authors.

As in our first book, *Your Work Matters to God*, we chose to write this one in Doug's voice because it's a more powerful way of communicating. It allows us to address you as a reader and as a person more directly. Nevertheless, be certain that this material is the product of a joint venture.

CHAPTER ONE

This Is a Book for Busy People!

If you're too busy to read this book,
you need this book!

"**I**'m too busy to read a book on time management!" you may be thinking. If so, you need this book!

My guess is that you've picked it up because somewhere, deep inside, you feel a gnawing conviction that things are getting out of control—and you'd like to regain control. You're hoping that this book can help.

It can! This is a book for people who are struggling with what I call the "too busies." Do you find yourself too busy to sit down and listen to your spouse talk about his or her day? Or too busy to play with your children as much as you'd like? Or too busy to relax and rest? Or too busy to think much about God? If so, you're suffering from the "too busies." Life is full of many demands, to be sure. But if you're too busy to attend to your marriage, if you're too busy to play with your kids, if you're too busy to detach from work and take time to rest, if you're too busy for God, *you're too busy!*

"I know," I hear someone crying, "that's why I want help!" Then this book is for you. It's for the person caught in crisis mode, whose goal is simply to get past the crisis of the moment, who feels victimized by the tyranny of the urgent. It's for the person who dashes from deadline to deadline, appointment to appointment, expectation to expectation, and—often—apology to apology.

Is there a better way? Yes! And this book will help you get started.

But first, a disclaimer: This is not a book about only time management.

Time-management books and seminars have their place. I know. I've been through my share of them. And I've talked with dozens of other people who've been through them as well. Like most of the self-improvement industry, such resources range from great to worthless, from very helpful to a total waste of time. Some promise and are able to deliver modest gains in getting control of your time. Many promise far more than they could possibly deliver!

At any rate, *this* book is not about time management. Certainly, I've included some principles of scheduling and so forth that are practical and helpful. But this book is about something much more fundamental, without which the greatest time-use strategies in the world would be like polishing the brass on the Titanic.

This book is about how to put your work in its proper perspective with the rest of your life. In fact, it's about how to honor Christ with your whole life, representing His values and direction as you pursue biblical balance in every area of your life.

Putting work in its proper perspective—is that something you need to do? I suspect it is; most of us need to. But I believe it's something we *must* do if we hope to live life as God intended!

Let me mention, though, a few symptoms that may suggest that you've allowed your life to get out of balance by letting work dominate and control you. You need to read this book if . . .

- You can't sleep at night because thoughts and feelings about work keep your mind in overdrive.
- Your spouse tells you something or asks you a question, and you realize you haven't heard a word of it because your mind is preoccupied with work.
- Your only serious reading is work related.
- You spend most of your time off at work, whether you're working or not.
- In your prayer life your only thoughts are about work.
- (Most significant!) You can't relax, or if you try to relax, you feel guilty.

"Well, in that case, this is a book for workaholics," I hear someone saying. "That's not me! I hate my job. It bores me. I guess this book is not for me!"

Wrong! This book is for anyone who has work out of perspective with the rest of life. You don't have to be a workaholic for that to happen. In fact, chronic boredom on the job is a good indication that you're not seeing your work as God sees it; you've come to regard it as a pointless but necessary evil, rather than a gift from God with great dignity and purpose.

That's really what putting work in its proper perspective is all about: dealing with the commitments and time demands associated with your job in the way that God intended. He never wanted work to eat up all of your life. Nor did He want it to be a curse that kills by boring you to death. Instead, He intended work to be held in balance with nonwork aspects of life.

What are the benefits of learning how to balance competing time demands? They're too numerous to list in full here. But as I've listened to hundreds, if not thousands, of individuals from the workplace who have struggled with this balance and are starting to achieve it, here are some of the typical comments I've heard:

• *"When I discovered that life is more than just work, I discovered life!"* Life is multidimensional. And our Creator desires that we enjoy and grow in every area of it, not just in work.

• *"This has restored me to my spouse and family."* After I had led a small group discussion on this material with a group of men, the wife of one of the men said to me, "Thanks for giving me back my husband!" Family relationships is probably the single most important reason why people who have lost control of their work want to regain control. They want their families back—and their families want them back!

• *"Learning to handle nonwork responsibilities just as I would work ones has given me a new sense of control over my life."* A life that is out of control is a life without hope. Work can become a crushing task-master whose demands are hopelessly relentless. But when work is put back into perspective and limits are enforced, and when nonwork areas are cultivated with the same discipline and intensity usually reserved for work, then we feel confident that we have some control over our lives.

• *"I find that I do a better job at work when I've paid proper attention to the rest of my life."* Nothing cripples like the feeling of having left something important undone. This is especially true for those of us who are task-oriented. But when we've attended to our important nonwork responsibilities (perhaps even at some cost to our careers), we find a release of energy that makes us more productive on the job.

• *"I now have a sense of God's approval, that He really is pleased with me."* As Christians, we *believe* that God accepts us unconditionally. But *feeling* that acceptance is hard, especially when work has us scrambling on a treadmill of expectations. Restoring a realistic balance to life can help rekindle a conviction that God is pleased with us. That's because we sense that we're living life as God intended.

• *"I've learned that my faith makes a big difference to my work."* Too many people see no relationship between their faith and their work. In fact, faith and work are often perceived as being in competition with each other. But when we see work from a biblical perspective, something wonderful happens: Our faith suddenly becomes extremely relevant to the issues and problems we face. Instead of seeing Christ as *opposed to* our work, we find Him involved with us *in* our work.

• *"It's meant such a relief from guilt."* Many workers stagger under an incredible load of guilt for their neglect of nonwork responsibilities and commitments. They know they should be placing limits on work demands. Yet they have so much emotional energy invested in their jobs that they can't detach from work, to the detriment of the rest of their lives. And so they feel guilty, as well as hopeless. How blessed is the person who is free to say "no" to the work monster that wants to eat up the rest of his or her life!

If you want to enjoy life-changing benefits like these—a sense of control and discipline, a sense of freedom and hope, a measure of progress in every area of life, a release from guilt, and a vision of God's smile upon your life—then I encourage you to read this book.

I want to help you put your work in its proper perspective with the rest of life. I've struggled with this problem, and allied myself with hundreds of other busy people struggling with it as well. Together, we've discovered that there is a way out of the swamp. We've discovered principles from the Bible that are helping us take small but steady steps toward the solid ground of a life under control—the healthy, satisfying life that God intends.

Let me begin, then, by introducing some of these people. You may find yourself in their stories.

PART ONE

Is Your Life Out of Balance?

CHAPTER TWO

We're All in This Together

No one escapes demands on his time.
Here are some examples.

Does anyone escape the relentless downpour of demands on his time? Not if he still has a pulse! Sure, some folks handle their schedules more efficiently than others; but in our culture, most of us get hit with a tidal wave of time demands every day. Here are three illustrations of what I mean.

FRANK

For months Frank had been wanting to spend more time cultivating his relationship with God. So one evening as he prepared for bed, he set his alarm for 5:30 a.m.

The alarm went off at 5:30. But Frank just turned it off, rolled over, and decided to catch a few more winks.

He was awakened, though, at 6:58, by the sun shining on his face and his wife's anxious voice: "Honey! It's 7:00 already! C'mon, get up! You're going to be late again!"

Again! Why did she have to insert that little word *again*? With a mixture of anger, guilt, and panic, Frank rolled out of bed and heaved a cup of coffee down his throat.

His eye caught an item in the sports section, and he began to scan it. Soon he was deeply engrossed, until he heard the nagging voice of his wife imploring him to get going.

With a growl Frank ran into the bathroom. Soon he had shaving cream all over his face and began to pull quickly at the razor. Suddenly, pink foam began to run down one side! He swore softly.

Somehow Frank threw his clothes on, grabbed his briefcase, and dashed for the car. As he nosed onto a clogged expressway, he recalled his vow to spend time with God that morning. Hoping to redeem himself, he decided to do some praying as he jockeyed through rush-hour traffic. So he turned the radio down to a background chatter and mumbled a few quick requests.

This strategy of prayer was punctuated by screeching tires and dirty looks, both given and received. Finally, as traffic thinned out, Frank got his car up to 70 or 75 mph, in a last mad dash to reach his office on time.

There he sneaked in the back door, avoiding his boss's office. At his desk, he pushed aside a Himalayan pile of clutter and began to hunt for the project he needed to finish yesterday. In the process he kept coming across pink slips with phone messages he'd forgotten about.

At this point Frank pondered how great it would be to do some basic thinking, planning, and prioritizing of his work. But that would take precious time. And Frank was already at a crisis point on several projects. So he just dove right in, scurrying like a madman between phone calls, memos, dictation, filing, and the men's room.

Shortly before noon, his friend Randall asked him to go to lunch. They walked to a nearby diner, where Randall proceeded to pour his heart out about his son, who was on drugs, and his wife, who was devastated by it. Frank would have liked to give a bit more time to Randall's problems. But he knew he had a meeting to get to, and since the boss was chairing it, Frank better not be late. He apologetically explained this to Randall, who nodded quietly and mumbled, "Yeah, I understand. Maybe some other time."

Back at the office Frank made it through the meeting by explaining that the project he was supposed to present was finished, but he just had to put some finishing touches on it. The boss wasn't smiling, but he seemed to accept this excuse. The truth was that Frank hadn't worked on that project since the last meeting!

That afternoon, Frank whittled the mountain of papers on his desk down to a manageable molehill. Then he was ready to get at that project. Before starting, though, he decided to take a break. So he headed down the hall and ran into a couple of his buddies. They started shooting the breeze, and forty-five minutes, three Cokes, and two Twinkies later, Frank decided he'd better get back to work.

But it was 4:45, and he promised his wife he'd be home by 5:30! So he worked as quickly as possible, not paying much attention to details. By 6:20, he was about done. Then he made a mad dash to the car for the chariot race home.

As he pulled in the driveway, Frank saw his children playing with their friends in the yard. He also saw a bike lying in the driveway—again! Exploding with frustration, he leaped out of the car, screamed at his kids, and tossed the bike aside. They stared at him blankly.

Inside, he gave his wife a token hug and noticed that the emotional temperature in the room was distinctly chilly. He mumbled an excuse about being late and a halfhearted apology, and slumped down at the table to eat a lonely, cold dinner.

While his wife put the kids down for bed, he flipped on *Monday Night Football*. By half time, he found himself hungry for a snack. Noticing his wife in the kitchen skimming the paper, he called out to her, "Honey, why don't you take a break and fix us a couple bowls of ice cream?"

For some reason he was surprised when she told him he could get his own ice cream! He thought about that and decided maybe she wanted attention. So he went out to the kitchen, gave her a hug, and started asking about her day.

At first she was very distant. But eventually she thawed and started spilling out details of a hectic day with the kids. He sort of listened as he dished out ice cream and shoveled it down.

But soon he realized that half time was over. So he interrupted his wife by saying, "Boy it really sounds like you've had quite a day! You know, we'll have to talk about it some more tomorrow." He said this while heading for the den, and the conversation ended.

The game went into overtime, but finally ended about 11:50. Frank was exhausted. He collapsed into bed with a sigh and soon was snoring soundly. Of course, he'd forgotten to set the alarm.

SHARON

The plaintive whine from the next room seeped through the cozy shell that enveloped Sharon. She snuggled deeper under the blankets, praying desperately that the little voice would go away, knowing for certain that it wouldn't.

Finally, ripped from the luxury of sleep by the necessities of motherhood, she threw back the covers and groped for her robe. Peering close to the dimly lit face of her alarm clock, she blinked and peered closer— 2:30 in the morning! A faint curse escaped her lips.

As she wandered down the hall, she brainstormed ways to prevent this sort of thing from occurring again: No juice before bedtime. Shorter naps at day care. No sleeping in the car on the way home. A bathroom visit before bedtime—whether it's needed or not.

But when she opened the door to Leslie's room, she immediately knew this would be no simple potty parade. The smell of sickness cut through the darkness, slashing to ribbons her plans, her expectations, her responsibilities for the next day. Once again this little person with the long brown braids and cinnamon eyes would demand the services of Sharon Johnson, mother and secretary, thereby disrupting the efficient operation of Long and Brown, Attorneys at Law.

Yes, of course they understood that she couldn't come in today. At least her boss said they did. But did they? Did anyone? Exactly what did they understand? That she was a mother? That she was therefore undependable? That she had a child who took precedence over any job commitments? That she cared more about her daughter than her job? No one said it that way, exactly, but she could hear it in their voices.

What they didn't understand was how desperately she wanted to excel in her work. She wanted to be competent, professional, and competitive. She wanted excellence. She wanted respect. In fact, she wanted to become a paralegal. Then she would have more status, more challenge, more opportunity—and more money.

But she couldn't get there from here. On her current salary she could never afford the extra schooling. Nor could she qualify for a loan. And even if she could, she would never be able to find the time for course work—or the energy. As it was, her days were filled with work and Leslie, Leslie and work. Nothing else. Nothing! Up at 5:00, dressed and ready by 6:00. Leslie up at 6:15, dressed and ready at 6:45, 7:00 at the latest. Then into the car (with a prayer that it would start). Drop Leslie off at day care by 7:30. Arrive at work by 7:45.

From there it was a scramble to keep pace with the two young lawyers determined to build a competitive practice. They ran a lean, mean shop. She especially felt the lean. And she knew they tolerated her occasional absences only because they couldn't afford better.

On the good days she got away by 5:00 or 5:15. Back to the daycare center by 5:30, check in hand on Fridays. ("Can you wait to deposit this until Monday," she'd invariably ask at the end of every month. "I've still got to get my paycheck to the bank!") Depending on traffic, they'd make it home by 6:15 or 6:30. She'd park Leslie in front of *Wheel of Fortune* while she threw dinner together.

After dinner the two would play with Leslie's stuffed animals, or read *Curious George*, or when Sharon could deal with it, make sugar cookies shaped like animals. Usually around 8:30 they would start the wrestling match of the bedtime routine. On good days it would be over by 9:00 with hugs and kisses and a little prayer. On the worst days it would be over by 9:15 with shouts and tears and smacks and a little prayer.

Then she faced the dishes, and picking up, and the mail. And exhaustion. With luck she'd drop into bed by

10:00 or 10:15. At least she could usually fall asleep immediately.

Weekends were a chance to play catch-up. The major chores like laundry, vacuuming, dusting, and cleaning the bathroom were sandwiched in between walks with Leslie, stories, games, and puzzles. Saturday afternoons or evenings were usually devoted to grocery shopping. And occasionally the two would have Linda and her little boy, Robert, over.

Sundays, of course, began with church, which Sharon appreciated because it gave her a brief break from Leslie and a few moments of adult stimulation. Sharon valued this interaction so highly that she tolerated the subtle distance she felt between herself and the many married couples. She also tolerated the lack of understanding her pastor displayed in his sermons—his hopelessly idealistic suggestions for Christian growth, and his seeming blindness to the realities she and others like her faced.

She did not feel bitter toward her pastor because of this, nor toward anyone else, at least not consciously—not bitter, but somewhat dehumanized, as if she were not a complete person. She had learned to accept a second-class status in life—in her church, in her occupation, in her family. It was not what was said that made her feel this way, but what was left unsaid, as well as the unspoken expectations that she could not hope to satisfy.

For Leslie's sake, Sharon accepted her lot. There were no other alternatives. She knew herself capable of far more—of that she felt confident. But the child was a liability—a bubbling, growing, endearing liability. And so Sharon's life was completely spent between the competing obligations of mothering and work.

That was why, when Mr. Brown accepted her sick

call by saying, "Of course, we understand," Sharon had responded by lying: "Thank you, Mr. Brown. I knew you would."

LUANNE

Luanne remembers the date, the time, and the place when she decided to return to the work force. It was a winter afternoon at 4:42, when her son, John, arrived home from school. She met him at the kitchen door and held out her hand. Mother and son exchanged a knowing glance, and the boy dug into his pocket with a defeated sigh.

Resigned to his fate, he drew out the slip of pink paper and handed it over. Then he stood silently, like a convicted criminal awaiting his sentence from the judge.

Finally the judge spoke: "Well, it's certainly an improvement over the last time. But what happened in history?" The youth shrugged and shook his head. "And this French grade is just . . . . Son, I know you can do better!" He nodded in meek agreement. "Well, we'll talk about it later when your father gets home."

Thus ended the inspection. But it was the last straw that pushed Luanne back into accounting. Her reasoning seemed simple and clear: college costs were already high and would go only higher. And there was just no way they could afford to send John and his little sister to decent schools on the modest income of her husband. Even if the company promoted him into the upper ranks of midlevel management—something you couldn't count on, with all the mergers and acquisitions of late—they would still never be able to afford it.

Furthermore, they probably couldn't rely on any scholarships for their kids. As this latest round of grades proved, the academic performance just wasn't there. Nor was her asthmatic son a standout in sports. Loans were a possibility, but she hated the thought of all that debt.

No, the only hope for college education for her two children would be if she took the plunge and returned to work. She knew she could easily find a job again, and she'd probably enjoy the change of pace.

At least she thought she would at the time. In reality, it had turned out to be a pretty big hassle. Not that she resented it. But after the initial excitement of new acquaintances, new surroundings, and new clothes wore off, she had settled into a predictable, and at times boring, routine. In the end, it was just a job—just a job to pay for college tuition.

Naturally, it meant some adjustments at home. Her husband was not delighted with her working, but accepted it with resignation as an inevitable reality of modern life. On the practical level it meant that dinner was sometimes late, and occasionally she brought work home or went to the office on weekends. He resented this intrusion of her job into family life, but tolerated it. He kept his mouth shut and learned to live with what he called her "accounting thing."

Her kids never really understood why she had gone back to work. John assumed it had something to do with her wanting to be as important as Dad. At least that's what his friends at school told him. And that seemed reasonable alongside the evidence of his social-studies class, where he learned all about equal rights for women and how important women were becoming in the work force.

His little sister, Shirley, perhaps guessed closer to the truth when she concluded it was about money. As she put it one afternoon to a playmate, "Mommy's got a job now, too, so we're going to have lots of money!" Perhaps that explained Shirley's constant nagging of her parents for this or that novelty from the shopping malls.

One thing both children immediately noticed was their mother's lowered energy level, especially at night. Luanne had always been a rather involved parent, not outgoing or vivacious, but aware of her children's needs and determined to supply those needs. They had known her as a dependable, steady parent whose stability had been a valued refuge in many storms.

Now she seemed grim and a bit fussy. She still got the job done. But her kids sensed a certain weariness, as though chores and routines that once had been simple and natural were now labored.

For Luanne, the situation carried so many ironies and unexpected feelings that she was unable to sort them all out. One Friday night at the end of a particularly hectic week, while Al was away on business, she reflected on her life. It struck her that the job she had taken to help her kids was becoming a barrier that kept her from enjoying more of their youth.

Yet her circumstances were no different from those of most of her friends. It seemed that they all worked—for many different reasons, to be sure. But one of the major reasons was always the money: it just took two incomes to make it these days.

That's why she found it odd when some of the younger women at her church spoke out against the idea of working mothers. They seemed so naive. Sure, she agreed that it would be best for preschoolers to have their mommies at home with them. And she was grateful that she and Al had been able to afford that luxury when John and Shirley were small. But now it wasn't really an option. So she dismissed the idealistic young mothers as simplistic. Give them ten years—or more like five—and they'd understand. They'd come around. They'd see how silly it was to ask, "But do you *have* to work?" They'd see that in this day and age, the answer for most mothers was a definite "Yes!"

I KNOW SOMEONE LIKE THAT

Perhaps you find something in common with Frank, Sharon, or Luanne, as they struggle to balance the demands of work and nonwork categories. They are by no means the only persons whose stories I could have related.

I could have told you about John and Estelle, a couple without children. He's a real-estate developer, she manages a public relations firm. Their struggle is to overcome the centrifugal forces created by work that tend to pull their marriage apart. Not that they want to end the relationship; in fact, they'd both like it to be stronger. But they are falling victim to what Sheldon Vanauken aptly described as "creeping separateness."

I could have discussed Alfredo, a single man in his early thirties, whose job as an investigator for a federal agency is all-consuming. Alfredo travels hundreds of thousands of miles each year, and being single with a good income, enjoys a comfortable lifestyle. But he has few real friends and no church involvement. What little free time he has is given to fixing up an old house he's purchased. His is a life of short-term commitments. It's also a life of temporary, fleeting satisfactions.

Then there's Larry, who works a day shift at a General Motors plant in Michigan. The hours and pay are decent, he feels. Still, it's "just a job." His real passion is hunting. And come deer season, Larry's boss finds him taking an unusual number of sick days, like the rest of his buddies. No one challenges them on this lapse, though. "After all," his boss figures, "you take hunting away from these guys, and life would be pretty boring."

Boredom is also a problem for Grace, who retired a couple of years ago from her job as a nurse in Portland. She misses the routine of the hospital. Her husband, also retired, seems only to want to sit around the house and read or watch television. Once a year Grace manages to nag him into flying with her down to Phoenix to visit her sister. But on the whole, Grace struggles with a loss of purpose since retiring. She has so much time on her hands, and would love to fill it up with meaningful, useful activity.

Still others could be mentioned: Dave, the professional athlete whose entire life is absorbed in his sport during the season, and with virtually complete freedom during the off-season; Alicia, the Ob/Gyn who lives her entire life "on call"; Jeff, the pastor who seems to be able to find time for everyone's needs and problems but his own and those of his family; Donna, the career homemaker, who feels more like a professional chauffeur and traffic cop than a mother and wife; or Harold, senior vice-president for a Fortune 500 company, responsible for a staggering number of commitments, yet deeply devoted to his wife of thirty years and their children and grandchildren, along with church, civic clubs, organizations, and a host of friends.

NEEDED: A PROPER PERSPECTIVE ON WORK

No amount of time-management strategies—as helpful and valid as those might be—can adequately address the one thing all of these people have in common: They all need to put work in its proper perspective with the rest of life. Naturally that will look different for each of them. Some need to set limits on work. Some need to pay more attention to it. But whatever specifics may be involved, they cannot hope to live a full, well-rounded healthy life, as God intended, unless and until they properly relate their work, along with the rest of their lives, to God.

The same is true for you. Work may or may not be all-consuming for you. It may or may not dominate your time and emotional energy—though I suspect that if you have picked up this book and read this far, it probably does. At any rate, if your life is out of balance in some way, and if you want to regain that balance, you'll need to start by considering where you might have taken a wrong turn in the first place. That's what we'll look at in the next three chapters.

I find that at least three fundamental mistakes, three wrong turns, can start a person down the road toward an imbalanced life. Furthermore, they can keep you gridlocked on that road of imbalance, such that you'll never find your way back. One of these detours is a secular view of work. That's what many Christians today have, believe it or not! A second dead end is a view of work promoted by many Christian teachers that actually distorts the Bible's teaching. A third wrong turn has to do with some personal character issues that can lead to disaster.

Before we consider what it means to balance competing time demands, I invite you to look with me at these three errant paths. In doing so, you may well discover some root causes of why your life may be out of control.

CHAPTER THREE

Are You Stressed for Success?

Our culture leaves God out of work—and gets work out of perspective as a result.

One of the surest and fastest ways I know to get life out of balance is to leave God out of your planning. "God?! What does God have to do with time management?" you may ask. And you may assume that the answer is "Nothing!"

That's exactly what most people assume in our culture today. And I'm sad to say, most Christian people do it as well. When they go to work, they leave God at home.

And why not? Does religion really have anything meaningful to contribute on the job? The work world is a tough, dog-eat-dog environment. Can Christianity really hold its own there? Can it stand the rigors of the street? I find that most people, especially most men, are skeptical as to whether it can. They regard God and the Bible and religion as irrelevant in the asphalt jungle.

It's not that people feel particularly negative toward religion. The vast majority of Americans believe in God, or at least in a Supreme Being of some sort. And overall church attendance is on the rise. So religion must have some value for people.

But not at work. When it comes to work, many people assume that religion in general and Christianity in particular have nothing major to contribute. They regard faith as a weekend hobby that appeals to some people, in the same way that golf or skiing appeal to others. Come Monday morning, it's time to put away our toys and get back to the "real world," as it's called.

That's a secular view of work. It's a view that just ignores God, that leaves Him out when the issue under consideration is work-related.

And it's a view that inevitably blocks us from enjoying life and work as God intended them, if for no other reason than because without God nothing in life is the way it should be.

TARGET FIXATION

I used to instruct fighter pilots for the Air Force in the Advanced Jet Training Program. One day I took a student up for his first real crack at handling evasive maneuvers. The idea was for us to fly out to the training area with a lead aircraft. Once there, lead would start at about 1000 feet in front of us to dive, climb, and turn in a series of maneuvers designed to throw us off his tail. My student's job was to stick with him.

I had noticed during the briefing that my student was nervous. But takeoff was normal, and he seemed to handle things quite well as we set up for our "dog fight."

At this point, lead was about three feet from us, doing 500 knots. On signal, the lead pilot began his maneuver with an abrupt turn away from us and a sharp dive about 50 degrees nose low. We waited a second or two, and then followed behind him at about 1000-foot spacing. The chase was on!

My student had performed this initial dive flawlessly. To anyone not familiar with supersonic flight it was a violent dive in which we screamed toward the ground. Recall what it feels like to come over the top of the first giant hill on a roller coaster. You leave your stomach at the top! Our dive was like that, except it felt like we left our *teeth* at the top!

The T-38 aircraft we used were both painted white. So at 1000-feet spacing, against the backdrop of the ground, lead was just a white dot on our canopy. But my student held with him. As we quickly descended, the altimeter whirred. In fact, our plane began to shake a bit, as it did whenever we approached supersonic air speed. The ground rushed toward us, and the canopy filled with a roar.

As I knew he would, lead suddenly executed a high-G climb, shooting like a star above us. As I saw that white dot climb higher and higher until it was out of sight, I waited for my student to follow. But he kept us in our dive!

My student's head seemed locked straight ahead. Sitting behind him, I realized he must have missed lead's evasive climb. So I asked him, "Lieutenant, do you have lead in sight?"

"Yes, sir, I do," came his confident reply. We continued our screaming dive.

"Well, where is he?" I asked in a slightly higher voice.

"He's in my twelve o'clock low, sir," he reported.

I sat up and looked out over my student's helmet to the position indicated. Sure enough, there in front of us was a tiny white dot. In fact, we were gaining on it rapidly. The only problem was that it was not lead. To my practiced eye, it looked to be a white oil tank!

With the tension of the flight, and in his inexperience, my student had fallen victim to what fighter pilots call "target fixation." Mistaking a white oil tank for lead, he had so fixated on it that he became oblivious to the surrounding phenomena that would have told him he was set on the wrong target.

I'm able to relate this story today only because I immediately grabbed the stick and pulled us out of the dive. I figure we were within fifteen or twenty seconds of what fighter pilots refer to as a very hot taxi! ·

THE WRONG TARGET

My student failed his ride that day because he fixated on the wrong target. In a similar way, many people today are fixated on the wrong target when it comes to how they live their lives.

God has already told us what He wants us to pursue as His creatures. He's indicated what the target in our lives should be. Yet, many people today are far removed from God's intention. In fact, they've abandoned God's objective; they're off pursuing targets of their own. To be specific, our present culture is dominated by *careerism*. People view their careers as the primary aim of life, and career goals as the most important goals worth pursuing. Success and significance are defined and determined today by career success and personal achievement at work.

A person can be an alcoholic, working on his third marriage, his kids might be on drugs, and his associates may hate his guts—yet if he's successful in his career, what do we call him? A success!

Of course, you don't have to be an alcoholic, or divorced, or have kids on drugs to be a careerist. All you have to do is let work eat up all your time and all your emotional energy. That's really what careerism does: it fixates us on the target of career achievements, so that we lose sight of other important aspects of life.

A friend of mine illustrates this well. He's the CEO of a large holding company with enormous assets. One day he invited me over to his office. As we talked, he proudly pointed to a row of notebooks on his mahogany bookshelf. Pulling one down, he showed me how it laid out specific plans for each of the company's very profitable ventures.

These notebooks were incredible! They had mission statements, action plans, and pro formas all neatly typed, categorized, and cross-indexed. They displayed enormously painstaking planning and thought. No alternative had been left to chance. They were an absolute masterpiece of strategic thinking, a blueprint for guaranteed success.

So what did my friend want to talk about? I finally asked. We sat down and he began to unburden his deep concern to have better relationships with his wife and kids. I asked a few questions to help me understand the situation, and then I asked him, "Hal, you obviously do a superb job at planning and setting goals for this company. Have you ever spent some time doing the same sort of thing for your family?"

You'd have thought I'd smacked him with a two-by-four! He was stunned! He just looked at me with a blank stare. For the reality was that he had *never even thought to do such a thing!* It was not that he was opposed to it; the idea simply had never occurred to him.

That's careerism. That's target fixation. That's becoming so focused on career goals and achievements that other critical areas of life—family, marriage, friends, health, even morals if necessary—go begging for time and attention. All commitments other than work commitments get sacrificed on the altar of career success.

THE IDOLATRY OF CAREER SUCCESS

For too many people, work has become a god that commands their devotion. When you think of an idol, you may imagine a piece of wood or stone in a jungle somewhere. But anthropologists define an idol as anything that becomes so sacred to us that it defines our self-worth, becomes the controlling center of life, and is the last to go in our list of priorities. By this account, work has become an idol for many people.

Think how much work defines who we are in this culture. We meet people and exchange greetings. Then, what's the first question we ask? "What do you do?" That is, what do you do *for work*? We're trying to establish who this person is and where he fits in society. Most importantly, we want to know what he's worth, and his job will give us clues to that.

Many of us want to know what someone is worth because it tells us what we're worth by comparison. Note that the follow-up questions are usually dominoes that fall with the answer to the work question. "Where do you live?" (That's determined by his income.) "Where do your kids go to school?" (Ditto.) "Who do we know in common?" (Relationships today are increasingly determined by work, so our mutual contacts will tell us even more about how we stack up.) And so on.

Depending on what crowd we're in, when we name the kind of work we do, we usually find either increased acceptance or subtle rejection. It often seems as if work establishes our worth.

It certainly controls the lives and priorities of countless people. Think back through the stories in Chapter 2. Or think about your own life. Does your job determine where you live, who your friends are, and how you spend your time? If you had a chance to make a million dollars, but knew it would probably cost you your marriage or your morals, would you go for the million? Suppose it were ten million, or a hundred million? How would your spouse answer that question? How are you answering it every day by your actions, your commitments, and your use of time?

A fixation on career success—whether that success is measured in dollars, power, applause, fame, votes, whatever—is a sure way to get life out of balance. That's because God never intended life to be devoted primarily to work. The same One who commanded, "Six days you shall labor and do all your work" (Exodus 20:9), prefaced that precept with the warning, "You shall have no other gods before Me" (Exodus 20:3).

No other gods. Has work become a god for you? If so, I urge you to tear down the altar of career achievement and replace it with a biblical view of success.

A BIBLICAL VIEW OF SUCCESS

We've seen how our culture defines success in purely secular terms as career success. Is there a biblical alternative? In Matthew 25:14-30, Jesus relates an intriguing parable about three slaves who were given management responsibilities by their master:

> "For it is just like a man about to go on a journey, who called his own slaves, and entrusted his

possessions to them.

"And to one he gave five talents, to another, two, and to another, one, each according to his own ability; and he went on his journey.

"Immediately the one who had received the five talents went and traded with them, and gained five more talents.

"In the same manner the one who had received the two talents gained two more.

"But he who received the one talent went away and dug in the ground, and hid his master's money.

"Now after a long time the master of those slaves came and settled accounts with them.

"And the one who had received the five talents came up and brought five more talents, saying, 'Master, you entrusted five talents to me; see, I have gained five more talents.'

"His master said to him, 'Well done, good and faithful slave; you were faithful with a few things, I will put you in charge of many things, enter into the joy of your master.'

"The one also who had received the two talents came up and said, 'Master, you entrusted to me two talents; see, I have gained two more talents.'

"His master said to him, 'Well done, good and faithful slave; you were faithful with a few things, I will put you in charge of many things; enter into the joy of your master.'

"And the one also who had received the one talent came up and said, 'Master, I knew you to be a hard man, reaping where you did not sow, and gathering where you scattered no seed.

'And I was afraid, and went away and hid your talent in the ground; see, you have what is yours.'

"But his master answered and said to him, 'You wicked, lazy slave, you knew that I reap where I did not sow, and gather where I scattered no seed.

'Then you ought to have put my money in the bank, and on my arrival I would have received my money back with interest.

'Therefore take away the talent from him, and give it to the one who has the ten talents.'

"For to everyone who has shall more be given, and he shall have an abundance; but from the one who does not have, even what he does have shall be taken away.

"And cast out the worthless slave into the outer darkness; in that place there shall be weeping and gnashing of teeth."

This story gives us great insight into what success means before God. Three employees are given a certain amount of money to manage. Two invest wisely and increase their shares. It's evident from every angle that they succeeded. Notice, though, that it's not really the money that matters to the master. Rather, it's their *faithfulness* that pleases him and causes him to give them increased responsibility. In both cases he says:

"Well done, good and faithful slave; you were faithful with a few things, I will put you in charge of many things; enter into the joy of your master."

The faithfulness of the first two slaves pleased the master and led to their success.

But, by contrast, notice the master's condemnation of the third slave. He calls the fellow "wicked" and "lazy"—just the opposite of "faithful." This incompetent slave displeased his master through his indifference to the master's instructions. He didn't even try to be faithful. As a result, the master dismisses him to utter ruin.

TRUE SUCCESS

This parable teaches us God's idea of success: *True success means faithfully pleasing God with the resources and responsibilities He's given us.*

That's a radical departure from what so much of our culture defines as success. And if we fixate on career achievement as the primary target of success in life, we'll completely miss God's joyful alternative. We'll be headed for a white oil tank, oblivious to the fact that we're way off course, headed for disaster.

That disaster may start as a life that shakes and rattles with imbalance and then starts coming apart. That's why I warn people whose work has consumed more and more areas of their lives: Beware! You're pursuing the wrong target. You've gotten work out of perspective. You need to return to a godly view of success.

But notice: What starts in this life as merely a preoccupation with work eventually ends in the next one with the condemnation of our heavenly Master. Could anything be worse? By contrast, could anything be more successful than to arrive in His presence and hear Him pronounce, "Well done, good and faithful servant! Enter into the joy of your Master."

That's the lasting joy I want. That's the truly satisfying success I want to experience. I hope you do, too. It comes from faithfully pleasing God with the resources and responsibilities He's given us in each area of our life.

We'll discuss how we can do that in Part Two. But before we get to that, we need to consider two other hindrances to balancing competing time demands.

CHAPTER FOUR

What They Don't Teach You in Sunday School

*Many Christians have been taught an
inadequate view of work—and that won't help
them keep life in balance.*

N ot long ago, Bill clipped an article from the paper
that featured an advertising executive who was
quitting his job to become a missionary in Africa. The
article told how this man had clawed and climbed his
way to the top in an extremely competitive field. And it
quoted him to the effect that "I had it all—money, status,
respect, power." But, he went on to explain, none of this
satisfied. None of it filled the empty void he felt inside.

This man was a Christian and had been a Christian
all through his career in advertising. So this was not a
salvation experience he was describing, but rather what
he termed "God's call on my life to serve Him."

He explained that in his "secular" job at the agency,
he'd been successful, yet dissatisfied. His work seemed
spiritually empty and meaningless. It provided abun-
dantly for his family, but impoverished his soul. This
inner void led him to a period of prayer and Bible study.

Then one day a denominational missions official
spoke in the man's church, and as he spoke, this fellow
felt God urging him to consider missions as a vocation.

Through a series of conversations and events, he quit his job at the agency and signed up for training as a missionary. That's the point at which the paper interviewed him and reported that he was on his way to Africa.

A FAULTY LOGIC

Now what are we to make of this man's story? Of course, we can't really question whether or not he should be going to the mission field. He feels that God called him to that work, and I certainly wouldn't and couldn't say that God did not call him. For all I know, missions may be exactly where this man belongs.

What I do question, though, is the process of reasoning whereby he quit his job at the ad agency. Even though he was a Christian during his tenure as an ad executive, he seemed to be approaching his work from a secular perspective. By his own account, he wasn't trying to please God and serve Him faithfully through his work in advertising. Rather, he seems to have left God out. His chief concern was with pleasing himself and satisfying his own career-oriented agenda. Like so many Christians, he had a secular view of work.

And that led, predictably, to a spiritual void that set him up perfectly for his decision to go into missions. He doesn't give us all the details, but I'd be willing to bet he reasoned it out like this: "I'm successful in my job, yet miserable in my life. Something's wrong! Maybe I'm out of God's will. In fact, I must be, if I feel so awful. I guess I'm just living for myself. But what would it mean to really live for God, to serve Him with my life, to do something that really counts for Him?

"Well, it would obviously mean getting out of advertising. That's a corrupt and corrupting environment. I should be doing something significant for God, like the ministry—sharing the gospel, teaching God's Word, devoting time to prayer. Yes, that's what I need to do! But where is the need greatest? We have so many churches here in our country. But they don't have so many in some places, like Africa. I think I'll give my life to God as a missionary in Africa!"

I can't prove that this man made his career change this way, but I do know that many others have thought and are thinking along these lines. But it's faulty logic. It's not a view of work and calling that's taught in the Bible. It's not that we don't need ministers and missionaries. We obviously do. In fact, we probably need far more than we've got.

But it's as wrong to go into the ministry with a distorted view of work as it is to work in an ad agency or any other occupation with a distorted view of work. Unfortunately, too many well-meaning Christians today and their teachers are misrepresenting what God has to say about work.

THE TWO-STORY VIEW OF WORK

Too many believers have bought into what I call a Two-Story view of work. Because Bill and I discuss this faulty perspective and its implications at some length in our book, *Your Work Matters to God* (NavPress, 1987), there is no need to discuss it in detail here. However, let me summarize by saying that the Two-Story view wrongly divides life into "sacred" and "secular" categories. "Sacred" activities are things associated with God and religion: church, Bible reading, prayer, evangelism, and the like. "Secular" categories include things with which God is presumably disinterested: hobbies, yard work, politics, sports, entertainment, and of course everyday work.

Having thus separated the activities of life into two spheres, the Two-Story view then sets up a hierarchy by saying that God values the "sacred" areas. These are things that "count" for God. They have "eternal value." They "really last." By default, "secular" areas are devalued as something beneath God's concern. They should be de-emphasized by those who want to really give their lives to God.

You can see right away how this view disparages everyday work. According to this view, work that matters to God is the work of ministry, evangelism, and missions. But if you drive a truck, program computers, sell insurance, or (God forbid) work in the financial services industry, your job doesn't count before God. In His eyes, you're a second-class citizen.

Is this a biblical view of work? Does it accurately represent God's perspective? With complete confidence we can respond: *absolutely not!* While this perspective may be widespread among some Christians, while it may claim many historical precedents, and while it may *sound* spiritual and "Christian," it's a distortion of the truth. Scripture shows us that work has *intrinsic* value because God Himself is a Worker and has created humans in His image to be His coworkers. Work is a gift from God, given to us at the creation, before the world knew sin and evil.

Furthermore, work has *instrumental* value, in that it serves at least five broad purposes, according to the Bible: (1) through work we serve other people and meet their needs; (2) through work we meet our own needs; (3) through work we meet the needs of our families; (4) through work we earn money to help the poor and those in vocational Christian work; and (5) through work we express our love for God.

If you carefully consider the biblical data, you have to conclude that everyday work matters to God. *Your* work matters to God! It matters to Him as much as the work of your pastor.

Enormous implications cascade out of this fundamental truth, but in this book we're interested in those that pertain to balancing competing time demands. And right away we can see that this alternative view challenges a very common notion about priorities.

A HIERARCHY OF PRIORITIES?

No doubt you've heard someone say, "In my life I put God first, family second, church third," and so on. Usually priorities four, five, six, and on down get rather fuzzy. But it's always God first, family second, and church third.

Now this sounds pretty good at first. If you're going to make a list of priorities, it seems reasonable to put God at the top. And family is awfully important. After all, if you're faced with a choice between guaranteed success in your career and holding your family intact, then according to the Bible, your family would have to take priority. You'd have to sacrifice career success to keep your family together. Church is important, too.

Does this hierarchy of priorities help you balance competing time demands and put work in its proper perspective with the rest of life? Maybe it does for you, but it doesn't do much for me. In my world, I'm rarely confronted with all-or-nothing choices. I can't recall the last time someone led me to a chasm where he held my wife in one hand and my contract in the other, and said,

"Okay, Sherman, which is it going to be—your wife or your job?" I'm not saying that will never happen. If it does, I may find the hierarchy to be of immense help.

But in the meantime, my choices are not so dramatic, though they are constant: Do I turn down a key career opportunity in order to spend more time with my kids? What if the survival of my organization and, therefore, my income depends on that opportunity? How about a request to teach a Sunday school class as opposed to sitting with my wife in the worship service? Or how about a chance to influence a political issue through membership on a civic committee as opposed to keeping my yard and my house well-maintained? Life is filled more with little tradeoffs than with life-and-death alternatives.

And what about simply trying to keep up with the enormously varied responsibilities, opportunities, and desires that require time commitments? Putting gas in the car. Coaching Little League. Calling a friend to say "Hi." Buying a new pair of pants. Taking out the trash. Reading the paper. Planning a business lunch. Negotiating with a computer salesman. Driving a child to the emergency clinic. Filling out tax forms. Cooking dinner. Attending a Bible study. Updating a voter registration card. Paying the paperboy. Settling an argument between the kids. Taking a call from your spouse. Waking up. Playing golf. Fixing a bicycle. Making travel arrangements. Reading this book. On and on.

God first. Family second. Church third. That's fine, but how does that list of priorities help us balance the many commitments that compete for our time? It doesn't. And the reason it doesn't is because this hierarchy of priorities stems ultimately from a Two-Story view of life and work. The Two-Story view is not found in Scripture; neither is the hierarchy.

Instead, the Bible gives us not a list of priorities, but a set of categories that we must balance under Christ's lordship. It's not family versus career, but family *and* career; not church versus work, but church *and* work; and so on. God is not simply the top priority in a list of responsibilities. He's the Lord of life who must be brought in on *everything* we do. We'll look in detail at this biblical balance of life in Chapter 6.

However, I think it would be appropriate at this point to mention a number of misconceptions people have about what a "biblically balanced" life looks like and how one gets there. I can't prove that these misperceptions stem directly from a Two-Story view of life, but I have found that in churches and groups where everyday work is disparaged and a hierarchy of priorities is taught, these mistakes invariably crop up. I call them fallacies of the Christian life.

FALLACIES OF THE CHRISTIAN LIFE

If your life seems out of control, if work is eating up more and more of your nonwork time, if you've gotten work out of perspective and want to regain that perspective, if you're reading this book in the hope that it will help you restore balance to your life—then I assume you're doing so out of a sincere desire to bring your life in line with God's intentions for living. You want to do things His way. You want to please Him. And you want to grow in your relationship with Him.

How does that happen? Suppose I accosted you on the street, shoved a microphone in your face, and demanded, "Quick! Tell me what Christian growth is all about. How does it happen?" What would you say?

Here's what people typically say when they answer that question. Their remarks display at least six fallacies of how Christians grow:

"I grow as a Christian by attending _____ church."
This is what I call the *attendance fallacy*. The idea is that as long as you make it to church regularly, or to Bible studies and other Christian-oriented programs, you're somehow growing as a believer. In fact, I know some pastors and others who evaluate the spiritual maturity of people in their congregations by how often they show up at church-sponsored events.

Now imagine your employer sitting you down for a performance review and saying, "Y'know, you really haven't done a very good job this year. You didn't fulfill your job description. You've neglected major projects. You've been a real pain to get along with. But you were here every day! I could count on it like clockwork. And I just so appreciate that, I'm going to award you a great big bonus!"

We can laugh at that. But it's no laughing matter to realize that many people expect to show up someday before God, attendance pins stretching from shoulder to shoulder, and hear His approval. They'll be shocked to hear His rebuke! Don't get me wrong, attending Christian programs and events can be helpful. But they are only a means toward a much greater end—the end of having a deep love for Christ and a character that acts more like Christ every day, in all areas of life.

"I grow as a Christian by doing certain activities."
This is the *activity fallacy*. The person with this view shows a laundry list of committee responsibilities, teaching assignments, and similar commitments that

keep her very busy in the cause of Christ.

Do these time demands help her grow? Do they keep her attitudes and values centered on Christ? Do they affect her character, so that she lives out a Christlike lifestyle at home and on the job? Do they promote intimate friendships with other believers, such that problem areas are dealt with and a healthy accountability is developed?

They may or may not. One thing is certain, though: They keep her *busy*! Whether all that busyness promotes true Christian growth is hard to tell.

It's sort of like a student pilot I was observing once while flying cross-country with him at supersonic speed. Halfway through the flight, I noticed we were way off course. So I asked him, "Lieutenant, where are we headed?"

"I don't know, sir," he replied, "but we're sure making good time!"

"I grow as a Christian by learning about the Bible."

This is a popular misconception that I call the *education fallacy*. The idea is that the more Bible knowledge you possess, the better off you are. Knowing becomes synonymous with growing.

The Bible does not teach this view, but a Hebrew concept in which "to know" is always "to know by experience." You don't *know* anything unless and until you do it. That's why James warns us: "But prove yourselves doers of the word, and not merely hearers who delude themselves" (James 1:22).

"I grow as a Christian by believing the right things."

Closely related to the education fallacy, I call this the *multiple-choice fallacy*. I find some people who act as if when they get to Heaven, God's going to give them a multiple choice exam on Christian doctrine.

Consequently, these people concentrate on understanding the finer points of theology. Unfortunately, they too often end up majoring in the minors. They can tell you everything about the problem of evil, but they ignore the homeless person. They wax eloquent on the heathen who've never heard the gospel, yet never mention Christ to their next-door neighbor. As one of my mentors puts it, they've got their ball lost in the weeds!

They are similar to the scribes and Pharisees whom Jesus castigated in Matthew 23:23-24:

> "Woe to you, scribes and Pharisees, hypocrites!
> For you tithe mint and dill and cummin, and have
> neglected the weightier provisions of the law:
> justice and mercy and faithfulness; but these are
> the things you should have done without
> neglecting the others. You blind guides, who
> strain out a gnat and swallow a camel!"

You can know the right answers, yet never become a more Christlike father or mother, never become a more godly employer or employee, never become a more biblical citizen, never become intimate with God. Christian growth is not doctrine; it's seeing our lifestyle change on a regular, ongoing basis.

"I can't say how a Christian grows, but I hope I will." This is what I call the *wishin'-and-hopin' fallacy*. The essence of this dead end is the perception that growth occurs for those who desire it enough. No real action plan is articulated, no real steps are taken. But somehow it'll happen!

Now let me ask: Would you run a business that way? "Boy, I sure hope we'll get some customers in here!" Are you doing any advertising? "Well, no, but I sure hope they'll come." Doubtful. "Well, I sure wish I could get my employees to show up to work on time!" Great, have you told them what the expectations are? Are there penalties for noncompliance? "Well, no, but I sure hope they'll change." Doubtful.

Spiritual growth is just as doubtful if it depends solely on having the right desires and dreams. Those who intend to follow Jesus can't just think about taking up their cross—they must actually take them up and follow Him. Sooner or later, good intentions must result in action.

"I grow as a Christian when I let go and let God."

This final fallacy is the *automatic-withdrawal fallacy*. It's the idea that somehow, mystically, with no effort on our part, God removes sin in our lives and makes us Christlike.

It's like an automatic-withdrawal program at a bank. Perhaps you have an insurance premium or some other recurring obligation that your bank pays for you by automatically withdrawing funds and paying the bill. It takes no effort on your part. It just happens— automatically.

Unfortunately, Christian growth doesn't work that way. Certainly we need to trust God with our lives, but we also need to take steps. We must let God do the things that only He can do, yet we must also do the things that only we can do.

The automatic-withdrawal fallacy is a lazy person's Christianity. It's the perspective of someone unwilling to accept responsibility for making choices and taking steps toward growing in Christlikeness.

If these six fallacies can't produce growth toward a balanced, Christlike lifestyle, what will? I'll present what I believe to be a more biblical model and a strategy in Parts Two and Three. But before getting to that, we need to consider one final set of problems that create a life that's out of balance. In the next chapter, we'll evaluate a cluster of personal issues that hinder us from living life as God intended.

CHAPTER FIVE

You Can't Get There from Here!

Three personal obstacles can deter you from enjoying life as it was meant to be lived.

No doubt you've heard the tale of the stranger in New England. Lost and confused, he finally came across a farmer and asked him, "Which way is it to _____?"

Scratching his head, the farmer looked down the road and began to explain. "You take this road about five miles, and then . . . well, no." He paused, and then turned in the other direction. "Okay, you go that way until you come to a big barn, then turn left. . .well, no, that won't work either." He thought and thought and tried a third tack. "If you head back the way you came, you'll pass a roadside stand. When you get there, take the left fork . . . no, that's not right." Finally, in frustration, the farmer threw up his hands and cried, "Son, you can't get there from here!"

If your life feels out of control even though you'd like to find a biblical, Christlike balance, it may well seem like you can't get there from here. Even if you don't have a secular view of work, even if you don't have a Two-Story view of work, and even if you've managed to avoid the fallacies of Christian growth—a cluster of personal issues can detour you into a cul-de-sac of defeat. And I can assure you that if any one of these issues grips your life, you won't get there from here! Let me describe three areas that are especially problematic for many.

REBELLION

When it comes to balancing time demands, one problem we all have lies not within our culture, nor within the Christian community, but deep within ourselves. It's the problem of rebellion. We are rebels at heart.

When I was a cadet at the Air Force Academy, it was the joy and delight of my life to break every rule I could. I don't like to admit this now, but I found myself breaking rules just for the fun of breaking rules. The fact that there were penalties for misbehavior only made rebellion more attractive.

Maybe testing the limits is just a characteristic of teenagers. But it's impossible to explain away the tendency of human beings throughout history and throughout the world today to resist obedience to authority. There's a rebellious streak in us that won't go away. What Isaiah prophesied concerning Israel is true for every one of us (Isaiah 53:6):

All of us like sheep have gone astray,
Each of us has turned to his own way.

Obviously this problem of rebellion affects far more than our use of time. It affects every other aspect of life. It even affects our eternal destiny.

But in regard to time demands, rebellion against God is catastrophic. When we resist God and tell Him, "Look, I'm going to live my life the way I see fit, and nobody's going to tell me what to do!"—when we do that, we run the grave risk that God may respond, "Okay, do it your way." We may get just what we ask for!

A man who found himself in this situation wrote me not long ago. He had been a high-level executive in a firm doing business with the Pentagon. His boss and others involved discovered plenty of ways to defraud the government. And even though this fellow was a believer, he decided that he knew more about how to run his life and his business than God did. So he compromised himself in an unbelievably complex web of felonies.

He got his way. He also got four years in prison. He also lost his wife and family, his entire life savings, his career, and four years of freedom. The only real things he gained from doing it "his way" were a felony record and a drug addiction.

He did gain one other thing: some much needed perspective on who God is. He learned that God is not a harsh, angry, legalistic taskmaster who gets some sick, sadistic satisfaction out of forcing us through ridiculous routines. Rather, God is the compassionate Creator who perceives the dark consequences of evil and sin, and who wants to help us avoid them.

Of course, rebellion against God may not land you in prison or get you hooked on drugs. But if left unchecked, it will inevitably place you in a hell of your own making. That hell may take the form of a broken marriage or even an intact marriage that lacks intimacy, little more than an arrangement between two strangers. It could be estrangement from your children that comes back to haunt you in the later years of life. It could be the perverse loneliness of prestige and status, by which people take no interest in you as a person, but merely in your wealth, your position, or your fame.

As C.S. Lewis put it, Heaven is the place where we say to God, "Thy will be done," and hell is the place where God says to us, "*Thy* will be done!" There's really only one way to avoid that hell—both for this life and the next. Whenever we find ourselves resisting God, we must swallow our pride, turn around, and start obeying Him. That's exactly what James 4:6-10 says:

> "God is opposed to the proud, but gives grace to the humble."
> Submit therefore to God. Resist the devil and he will flee from you.
> Draw near to God and He will draw near to you. Cleanse your hands, you sinners; and purify your hearts, you double-minded.
> Be miserable and mourn and weep; let your laughter be turned into mourning, and your joy to gloom.

This is a change of attitude. However, what starts as a change of attitude must go on to a change of behavior. (We'll look at that more later in this book.) But there's a second problem that keeps many of us from living life as God intended. It's the old problem of procrastination.

PROCRASTINATION

At the end of Proverbs 24 is a little snapshot loaded with insight into the problem of procrastination. Verse 30 begins: "I passed by the field of the sluggard, and by the vineyard of the man lacking sense."

The owner of the field is called a sluggard, so people assume this is a proverb about laziness. It is, but as we'll see, laziness is really just a part of procrastination. At any rate, this fellow who owns the field lacks sense. In other words, he's living foolishly.

Here's why. Having grown up in the city, I don't know a lot about agriculture. But I'm told that a vineyard, which is what the man in this passage had, takes more work and care and attention and diligence than just about any other sort of farming. Has this farmer cared diligently for his vineyard?

> Behold, it was completely overgrown with thistles,
> Its surface was covered with nettles,
> And its stone wall was broken down. (verse 31)

How bad was this vineyard? Well, let's just say it probably wouldn't have made *In Search of Excellence!* It must have looked like my front yard! The vineyard did not have just a few weeds here and there, showing a little bit of neglect; it was "completely overgrown" with weeds, showing total neglect.

Furthermore, the protective wall surrounding the vineyard was in ruins. So what little fruit the vineyard produced was at the mercy of foxes and other thieves, both animal and human.

What would you conclude, looking at the situation? Probably the same thing as the writer:

> When I saw, I reflected upon it;
> I looked, and received instruction.
> "A little sleep, a little slumber,
> A little folding of the hands to rest." (Proverbs
>   24:32-33)

Looking at the field, you can guess the owner's attitude: "Our goal is to get a good night's sleep, plenty of naps, and lots of coffee breaks."

Now, there's nothing wrong with sleep or relaxation. In fact, Psalm 127 encourages it. But the point in Proverbs 24 is that through his excessive indolence, this fellow was on a path to sudden and unexpected disaster. Notice how the story (and the farmer) ends:

> Then your poverty will come as a robber,
> And your want like an armed man. (verse 34)

No one ever schedules a burglary. Robbers don't come that way. They come suddenly, dramatically, when they're least expected. And that's what happened to this man. He kept putting off the attention his field deserved, putting it off so he could catch a few more winks, a few more beers with the boys. Then suddenly—it was over. He lost his field, he lost everything.

Procrastination is the path to sudden and unexpected disaster. And it's not just a problem for biblical farmers.

At one time there was a man involved in our program who let his work eat up more and more and more of his life. When he stopped attending some luncheons we were sponsoring, I didn't think much of it. I knew that busy people have to set limits somewhere.

But then he started staying at work later and later, neglecting his wife and children. He told them it was just a temporary thing—just six or eight months. After all, it was a period when the economy was booming, and he wanted to ride the rocket all the way to the moon. In fact, he told them it was for *their* benefit. After he made a killing, he explained, he would be able to cut back and give them the attention they deserved.

Soon it became weekends at work too. In fact, this

man's entire life boiled down to his job and a Sunday school class he taught. (Some example for a Sunday school teacher!) For months this dragged on as his industry broke all-time records. So he never did get around to focusing on his family.

Well, one Friday night his wife nagged him into taking a break and going out to dinner with another couple. Reluctantly, he went, and it turned out that they had a great evening. In fact, as he and his wife retired for the night, he thought about how his life couldn't be better.

At 7:00 the next morning, this man awoke to find movers in his bedroom. Uniformed guys were packing up boxes, hauling furniture, and rolling up carpets. In fact, they asked him to get out of the bed so they could dismantle it.

Startled, he scrambled out of bed and staggered down the hall where his wife was directing traffic. He demanded to know what was going on, at which point she handed him a sheaf of papers—divorce papers and a court injunction forbidding him from contacting her or the children for a period of time. She was leaving him and taking the children and the furniture. He could have the house.

Procrastination is the path to sudden and unexpected disaster. That's an extremely important principle for balancing competing time demands. I know so many people who have been exposed to the ideals of Scripture, yet never really do anything about them. Oh, they tell me they're going to follow them—someday!

If that's your line, let me encourage you to start changing your life *today*. If your marriage has problems or needs attention, start doing something about it *today*. If your attitude toward a coworker stinks, do something to change it *today*. If you've compromised your ethics on the job, start making amends *today*. Whatever your area of need, start working on it *today*.

You can't fix everything that needs fixing in one day, but you'll never fix anything until you get started. Your life may be in such disarray that it looks like the vineyard in Proverbs 24—completely overgrown with weeds. You won't get rid of all those weeds in a day or a week. But right now you can start pulling one or two of them. Where would you like to begin?

DISCOURAGEMENT

Of course, if your life is completely overgrown with weeds, you may fall prey to a third condition and that's discouragement. I know people who feel completely hopeless about their lives. And, I have to admit, sometimes when I look at the straits they're in, I feel discouraged for them!

But discouragement is largely a matter of perspective. As a human being, Jesus felt many emotions but one that we never see or hear about is despair. Even in the Garden of Gethsemane, faced with death, He never lost hope. Why? I'm convinced it was because He never lost sight of His Father. And nothing can instill greater confidence and hope—no matter how bad the circumstances—than the presence of a heavenly Father who is in control and who treats you like a very loved son or daughter.

That's who our heavenly Father is. Hebrews 12:7 assures us, "God deals with you as with sons [or daughters]." God is fully aware of all the weeds in our lives—all the problems, all the needs, all the hurts. He knows that some are the result of poor choices on our part, some are the result of injuries inflicted on us by others, and some are just part of life in a fallen world. But whatever the source of our difficulties, God loves us too much to leave us at their mercy.

I can't predict exactly how God will right all the wrongs in your life. But when it comes to balancing competing time demands, I find that for most people it's a matter of trusting God *and* taking steps. We have to trust that indeed God knows the way out of the swamp, but at the same time we have to take whatever steps God may indicate.

At this point you may throw up your hands and wail, "Oh, I've tried time and again to get my schedule under control, but it's no use! Sooner or later, I always slip back into my old ways."

If that's your situation, let me point out the reality that life is tough, and we as humans are weak. Some people are stronger in some areas than others, but none of us, apart from God, is stronger than our ultimate enemy, which is sin. Fortunately, God knows that this is the situation.

> The LORD is compassionate and gracious,
> Slow to anger and abounding in lovingkindness.
> He will not always strive with us;
> Nor will He keep His anger forever.
> He has not dealt with us according to our sins,
> Nor rewarded us according to our iniquities.
> For as high as the heavens are above the earth,
> So great is His lovingkindness toward those who
>   fear Him . . . .
> For He Himself knows our frame;
> He is mindful that we are but dust. (Psalm
>   103:8-11,14)

What a picture: a loving Father aware of our circumstances and aware that we are of a weak frame. According to this psalm, the only way we can avoid God's compassion is by not fearing Him (recall the earlier discussion about rebellion).

If you're feeling discouraged about your progress in the Christian life, let me encourage you that God is delighted, in fact, He's ecstatic, over *whatever* steps you take toward Christlikeness, the way any parent delights in the first, faltering steps of his or her baby.

Recently I had a virulent case of the flu, probably as rugged a bout as I've ever had. For days I was miserable. One of my sons decided to encourage me, so he got out some markers and paper and drew me a picture of a fighter jet. I'll bet he spent an hour or two on that picture. And then he brought it to me.

That drawing might not look like much to you, but to me it meant everything in the world! I was overjoyed. The juvenile quality of the art was completely lost in the bond that was built between me and my son. He had done something to please me, and I was thoroughly pleased with him.

That's what passages like Psalm 103 and Hebrews 12 tell us about God. He's so pleased with whatever meager steps we take that it's really less important what those steps are than that we take them. The wonderful thing is that if we keep taking them, if we keep walking toward Christlikeness, we'll make significant progress.

One caution, though: In taking steps and measuring your progress, beware of becoming a Christian perfectionist. I know people who are gravely discouraged because they're not spending four hours a day in prayer, as Martin Luther did. No, they're spending only one hour!

Can you imagine that—an hour a day in prayer, and they're discouraged! That makes no sense to me. Most of us would do well to get up to five, or ten, or fifteen minutes a day praying. So to be neurotically critical of yourself when you make room for only an hour is to be terribly unrealistic in your expectations.

It's true that our ultimate standard is Jesus, and He was perfect. But consider: Moses was not perfect; he was a murderer and a coward; yet he was called "the friend of God." David was an adulterer, a murderer, and a lousy father; yet he was called "a man after God's own heart."

How could this be? The answer is that while perfection is the standard, the One doing the measuring is filled with gracious compassion. He knows we are weak and frail and imperfect. So instead of berating us for our imperfections, He encourages us to make one small step at a time toward Christlikeness. He is less interested in the velocity of our progress than in its direction, less in how much time we're spending in prayer than in the progress we're making in our prayer life.

Rebellion, procrastination, discouragement. Three roadblocks you'll want to avoid if you intend to put your work in proper perspective. But what is a "proper perspective" on work? What does it mean to "balance competing time demands"? We'll find out in Part Two.

PART TWO

What Does It Mean to Balance Competing Time Demands?

CHAPTER SIX

The Pentathlon: A New Way of Looking at Life

*The Bible teaches a comprehensive view of life
that helps us keep things in perspective.*

If you sign up to play a sport in high school or college, the coaches use a lot of recruiting strategies to get you on the team and keep you motivated. Unfortunately, they don't tell you that at some point you'll have to sit through a sports banquet.

Maybe you've attended one of these affairs. All the athletes look a bit sheepish in coats and ties, and everyone chokes down a chunk of old tire disguised as chicken. Awards are handed out. And then a grizzled veteran of the sport (who was a big name in your grandfather's day) gets up and tries to say something intelligent.

Usually the speaker is just a good guy being asked to impersonate a philosopher. So he does his best. He tells a few jokes and runs through his repertoire of stories about the game. Finally, trying to inject some semblance of meaningful substance into the evening, he tosses out a cliché that he feels summarizes life: "It's not the starters who win in life, it's the finishers," or "A man isn't measured by what he has, but by what he does with what he has," or "Whatever the mind can conceive, the will can achieve."

I think most of us recognize how simplistic such folk wisdom is. Hardly enough to cover all the bases in life! We feel skeptical because we know that life is complex, and it's lived very differently throughout our society, let alone the world. This is especially true for the issue of work. Different cultures, and certainly different individuals within cultures, see work and value it in vastly different ways.

That being the case, I want to avoid simplistic formulas in my efforts to help you balance your life. I've already said that my purpose in writing this book, ambitious as it may be, is to help you put work in its proper perspective with the rest of life. And as soon as I say that, I'm reminded of just how difficult a task that is.

What can I offer, therefore, that will be universally true and have broad application?

Fortunately, I have a resource in the Bible, which I take to be God's authoritative written revelation of Himself and His truth. While the Bible was written in the context of certain cultures, its truths are universally and eternally true—that is, they are true and apply to you and to me today just as much as they did to those living at the time they were first recorded.

So when I speak about "a biblical view of work" and of "putting work in its proper perspective with the rest of life," I don't need to give you only my opinion and hope that works for you. Rather, I can invite you to look with me at what God has said in His Word about work and about where it fits into life. Then we can discuss how that truth might apply to us in the culture in which we live and work.

In this chapter and the next, I want to examine the

Bible's perspective on work as a part of life. Then in the remainder of the book, we'll talk about ways to apply that perspective in practical terms.

A MODEL OF LIFE

In Chapter 4, I mentioned that many Christians talk about their lives and their priorities in terms of a hierarchy: God first, family second, church third, and so on. I said, rather emphatically, that while this listing has some value, it's not really a view of life taught in the Bible (even though it may sound like it ought to be).

In that case, we might reasonably ask, what is the view of life taught in the Bible? That's not an easy question to answer, because we don't have one main passage in Scripture that begins, "Here's how you should look at life." That's probably because life is complex.

Still, when we go to the Bible to find out where work fits in, we learn that work is one of a number of categories that are addressed over and over, categories that are common to everyone's life. As I observe the data, I find five main areas addressed:

1. *Personal life*, including one's relationship to God, one's emotions, and all of the private, individual, inner aspects of one's life.
2. *Family*, including one's spouse (if married), children, parents and other extended family, and any dependents.
3. *Work*, that is one's employment or occupation, how one earns a living (for career homemakers, homemaking is their work).
4. *Church* life, by which I mean one's relationships both near and far to those in the family of God.

5. *Community* life, by which I mean one's responsibilities as a citizen toward the government and one's relationships in the broader society and the world, especially with those outside the faith.

The Bible addresses a *comprehensive view of life.* And what is most important for our discussion is that work is only one of the five categories. Work is not all of life. Nor is it a minor detail of life. Nor is it a necessary evil in life. It is a major category that must be kept in perspective with the other four.

THE PENTATHLON

In Europe, one of the most prestigious and demanding of athletic contests is the pentathlon. Perhaps you're familiar with the decathlon in our country and in the Olympics, which has ten events to it. But the pentathlon requires an athlete—a pentathlete—to compete in five events: a 4000-meter cross country race, a 300-meter freestyle swim, a 5000-meter, thirty-jump equestrian steeplechase, pistol shooting at twenty-five meters, and épée fencing.

Can you imagine just being able to do all five of these activities, let alone competing in them with athletic skill! From time to time I enter a triathlon, where I must ride a bike for twenty-four miles, swim about a mile, and then run a ten-kilometer race (about six miles). That's a three-event competition that tests endurance more than it does skill.

But the pentathlon measures finesse as well as strength. Think of the diversity those five events require. Speed and power alone won't win. Nor will technique and skill. Nor will strategy and experience. No, it takes all this and more to win the pentathlon. It's a true test of one's overall abilities.

This pentathlon is a useful image to understand the Bible's teaching regarding the five categories of life mentioned earlier. In fact, I call this biblical model the Pentathlon. Let me describe what I mean.

The pentathlon is comprehensive: to win, you must do well in all five events.

As a pentathlete, you can't do exceptionally well just in one or two areas, like running and swimming, and blow off the other areas just because you don't like horses or you have a thing about handguns. You have to excel in all five areas.

In a similar way, the Bible doesn't allow us to major in just one or two categories of life—say in our personal life, or in our work. I know some people who think God is totally impressed with the fact that they have a superb time of worship and prayer each day. Prayer and worship are commendable, but if people neglect their responsibilities toward their employer and their obligations as citizens, then biblically they're off base. It's good that they're doing so well in one area—but there are four others to pursue.

Likewise, if you're excelling in your work to the glory of God, that's fine. But don't forget that God also expects you to please Him in your personal life, in your family, in your church, and in your community. To "win" in the biblical Pentathlon, you must pursue growth in all five areas.

The pentathlon requires you to develop diverse skills.

It takes speed and strength to run and swim effectively. It also takes coordination. Horseback riding requires balance and timing, to say nothing of knowing how to work an animal. Pistol shooting calls for unusual hand-eye coordination and steady nerves. And fencing (according to Bill, who has done it) requires strategy, lightning speed, dexterity, an almost ballet-like nimbleness, and the prescience to anticipate your opponent's next move. We could add to this list of abilities the mental talents of judgment, competitive savvy, the knack of predicting outcomes, the ability to size up the competition, and the genius of pacing and timing.

In short, the pentathlete must be a superb specimen of humanity! Every facet of his body and mind will be tested in competition.

The biblical Pentathlon is no different, because life is so diverse and requires a variety of skills. Think, for instance, what different talents it takes to succeed in the workplace than in the home. The arena of work is a task-oriented environment. The business world in particular is sometimes a competitive jungle where true thoughts and feelings are often hidden and where numbers seem to reign supreme. Contrast that to the home, which is (or should be) relationally oriented, inclusive, open to expressions of ideas and emotions, and marked by love and acceptance. To master both work and family will take an enormous range of skills. And if by chance someone should master them, there are three other aspects of life requiring even more diverse skills.

To compete effectively, you must plan your preparation carefully and coordinate your training.
If winning requires excellence in all five events, and if each of the events requires vastly different skills, then the pentathlete must use his limited training period very strategically. He must know himself well, his

strengths and weaknesses, and apportion his preparation accordingly.

The same is true for you as a Christian. If you're single, you'll approach the biblical Pentathlon very differently than if you're married and have children. Likewise, if you have a part-time job and attend night school, your approach will look very different than if you're an orthopedic surgeon who is constantly on call.

The beauty of the Pentathlon concept is that it takes individuality into account. Each believer has a unique walk with God. Consequently, each of us must answer to God for how we respond to Him in each of the five areas, knowing that our approach may be very different from someone else's.

In the pentathlon, each event affects every other event. Suppose I were a pentathlete and spent all my training time on fencing. I'd probably excel in fencing, but do poorly in the other areas. The only way around this problem is to strike a strategic balance in my training between all five areas.

Likewise in the Christian's Pentathlon, every area affects every other area. What I do privately affects my work, my church, my family, and my community. What I do at work affects everything else. If I get out of balance in one area, I lose balance throughout my life.

Consequently, in order to please God throughout my life, I must strike a strategic balance among the five areas of the Pentathlon. By a "strategic balance" I don't mean carving up your 168-hour week into five equal slices of 33.6 hours each. That would not be a strategic balance—that would be a mess!

No, a strategic balance means a carefully considered assessment of where you—as a unique individual—need to put your time in order to faithfully please God with the resources and responsibilities He's given you. One place I strongly suggest you start that assessment is with a realistic determination of how much time you need to spend at work. That's because for so many of us, work seems to be the area that most easily gets out of hand.

There's nothing sacred about a forty-hour work week. Exodus 20 talks about six days of labor, which in an agrarian economy could amount to an eighty-hour week. The point is, evaluate your job, your profession, your options, and yourself, and make a realistic appraisal of the time it will take you to satisfy the requirements of your position. This may help you set realistic limits on your work, so that you can adequately and appropriately attend to the other responsibilities you have before God.

Remember, life is interrelated and dynamic. I've represented the five categories of the Pentathlon as though they were five mutually exclusive parts of life, but actually they overlap considerably. Whatever plans, commitments, and changes you make in one area will affect the other areas. Keep that in mind as you try to find your strategic balance.

No athlete ever arrives at perfection in any event.
No matter how many times a marksman hits the bull's-eye in pistol shooting, he still must practice and prepare for that event, because he always stands a chance of shooting wide of the mark. He'll never get to the point where he can guarantee he'll hit the center of the target 100 times out of 100.

Nor would he practice that event to the point where he could, because then he'd have to neglect the other four events. No, the way he improves is to set limited goals in each of the five areas and then strive to meet those goals. Once he does, he sets new goals. In this way he moves step by step toward excellence—but never to perfection.

In the Christian life we'll never "arrive," we'll never become "perfect and complete, lacking in nothing." But what we can do (and what I'll show you how to do in Chapter 11) is to set limited goals in each of the five areas of the Pentathlon. In that way we can take small, but important, steps toward Christlikeness.

The point of the pentathlon is the goal of winning.

If the pentathlon requires as much skill and preparation as I've described, then what would motivate someone to seriously train for it and compete in it? I'm sure that if we could ask a pentathlete that question, he'd have a lot to say about his personal motivation and purpose in competing. But what he would have in common with every other serious contestant is the overall aim of winning the pentathlon.

Similarly, in the life the Bible describes, the central integrating point is Jesus Christ. All the skills, all the disciplines, all the strategies are merely means toward knowing Christ, pleasing Christ, loving Christ, following Christ, becoming like Christ. You may enjoy many benefits from living according to the Bible's teaching, such as inner peace, a sense of purpose and meaning, or a stable home life. But these are just byproducts of the process. The *goal* of living, according to the Bible, is an intimate relationship with Jesus Christ. This was Paul's conclusion as described in Philippians 3:7-8:

> But whatever things were gain to me, those things I have counted as loss for the sake of Christ. More

than that, I count all things to be loss in view of the surpassing value of knowing Christ Jesus my Lord, for whom I have suffered the loss of all things, and count them but rubbish in order that I may gain Christ.

In fact, earlier in that same letter, he declared, "For me, to live is Christ" (1:21).

THE BENEFITS OF THE PENTATHLON

Looking at life and work from the perspective of the Pentathlon yields at least four benefits.

First, the Pentathlon model contrasts sharply with the secular view of work described in Chapter 3. Recall that when a person leaves God out of her work, she opens herself up to making an idol of her career, of equating success in life with success at work.

By contrast, the Pentathlon properly relates our work, along with the rest of our lives, to God. Since Christ is Lord over all of life, He is Lord over work, too. And the encouraging thing is that when we go to the Bible, we don't find it ignoring our day-to-day work activities. Rather, it devotes considerable teaching to those very important activities. So we need not leave God at home when we go to work.

This brings us to a second benefit of the Pentathlon model. Recall that in Chapter 4, I described the Two-Story view of work, which says that because work is "secular," it doesn't matter to God. But in fact, work *does* matter to Him, because it is one of five major categories of life. Because Christ is Lord over all of life, He is Lord over our work.

This is a blow to the hierarchical priority system that

is so casually promoted among Christians. If we're going to have a list, Jesus shouldn't be at the top of the list; He shouldn't even be on the list! That's because He's not just another item, another responsibility, another entry on the checklist. He's the Lord of life, whom we should seek to please whether we're kneeling in prayer, negotiating a sale, or casting a vote. "Whatever you do," Paul tells us, "do all in the name of the Lord Jesus" (Colossians 3:17). We're not to serve Jesus first, then serve our family, then serve our church, and on down a list. We're to serve Jesus *as* we serve our family, our church, our work, our community, and our own needs.

A third benefit, then, is that the Pentathlon integrates life into a comprehensive whole under God's direction. Christians do not need to be fragmented, mechanistic, schizophrenic people rushing neurotically from one activity to another. Instead, we can pursue a well-rounded, healthy life that sets limits, yet enjoys the freedom that comes from balance.

Finally, the Pentathlon offers us a model of life that fits naturally with our own experience and with the teaching of Scripture. In presenting the Pentathlon, I'm not proposing some new, weird approach to life by which you have to learn a new vocabulary and get rid of your friends and join some group with special knowledge. The Pentathlon simply accepts life the way most people throughout history and around the world today live it: they all have personal needs and concerns, they all have families, they all have religious questions and interests, they all work, and they all must relate to some wider community.

Furthermore, you don't have to wrench the biblical data out of context to find the Pentathlon. You don't have to do fancy Hebrew and Greek word studies or theological gymnastics to find it. It simply emerges from the Bible. And it's to this last point that I want to turn in the next chapter. I want us to feel certain that in adopting the Pentathlon as a way of seeing life, we're indeed looking at life from God's perspective.

CHAPTER SEVEN

But Is the Pentathlon Valid?

*Don't take my word for it. The Pentathlon is
right out of the Bible!*

In recent months the headlines have been buzzing with scams from Washington to Wall Street to Heritage U.S.A. But the king of the cons was Charles Bianchi, later Charles Ponsi, who in late 1919 turned up in Boston as Charles Ponzi, formerly of Montreal.

Mr. Ponzi set up an investment firm with the reassuring name of The Securities and Exchange Company. He promised the intelligent citizens of Boston that in ninety days he could return their cash with forty percent profit! Needless to say, business was as brisk as a blizzard can be. So much cash was dumped on him that Ponzi soon upped the profit on ninety-day notes to one hundred percent, and introduced forty-five-day notes at fifty percent!

This financial avalanche continued until August of 1920, when government bloodhounds began baying. An audit revealed that Ponzi had actually invested a mere $30 of what he took in! As for the rest, he had paid off early investors with cash donated by later ones. Meanwhile, the press, retracing his steps to Montreal, found a legacy of fraudulence crowned by a prison term.

Ponzi eventually died a pauper. But his name lives on in the term "Ponzi scheme." John Train, a Manhattan investment attorney, defines this as any business proposition that offers more than there can possibly be in a given situation. It's an investment opportunity that offers something for nothing, yet in the end delivers nothing because it is based on nothing. It's an empty promise—a sham and a scam.

I find a parallel in a lot of religious teaching today that claims to be "biblical." Certain schemes and ideas for Christian life and growth are spiritual Ponzi schemes: at a glance they look and sound great. But upon close inspection (of the Bible), they are found to be without credible support. Furthermore, experience shows them to be bankrupt; they're like worthless checks—you can't cash them in.

But of course in the last chapter, I described the Pentathlon, which I called a "biblical" model for life. Is it? Or am I just proposing one more spiritual Ponzi scheme that sounds intriguing, but on inspection and by experience only dashes one's hopes? In this chapter I want to show that the Pentathlon is biblical because: (1) it helps us honor God in every aspect of life; and (2) because the biblical text clearly addresses the five categories of the Pentathlon.

A COMPREHENSIVE VIEW OF LIFE

How did the Hebrews in the Old Testament look at life? As we study the text and try to make out the big picture, it becomes apparent that while they regarded certain things as sacred, they saw life as a comprehensive, unified whole. The unifying principle was that everything in life was to be related to God.

To be sure, they talked about aspects of worship and religious ceremony with words like "clean" and "unclean," "holy," "acceptable," "consecrated," and "sanctified." Yet they never saw God as being divorced from or unconcerned with day-to-day affairs. In fact, they saw Him as the Lord over *all* of life. It was not just worship and ritual that mattered to God. He was also deeply concerned about ethics in the marketplace, justice in the courts, victory in the military, discipline and love in the home, and the character of the individual. *Every* element of life was to be lived as unto God.

An outstanding example of this comprehensive, unified view occurs in Deuteronomy, the "Second Law," in which God commanded parents to cultivate a love of Him in their children, by weaving Him into the warp and woof of everyday life:

> "Hear, O Israel! The Lord is our God, the Lord is one!
>
> "And you shall love the Lord your God with all your heart and with all your soul and with all your might.
>
> "And these words, which I am commanding you today, shall be on your heart; and you shall teach them diligently to your sons and shall talk of them when you sit in your house and when you walk by the way and when you lie down and when you rise up.
>
> "And you shall bind them as a sign on your hand and they shall be as frontals on your forehead. And you shall write them on the doorposts of your house and on your gates."
> (Deuteronomy 6:4-9)

Every detail of life was to be related to God. While the ceremonial, religious aspects of the Hebrew culture were termed holy, in a sense, all of life was to be holy, because every aspect of it was to be lived with a love for the Almighty.

So what does all this have to do with the Pentathlon? Simply this: I believe the Pentathlon (which emerges specifically from the New Testament, as we'll see) reflects the balanced, comprehensive view of life under God's lordship as taught by the Old Testament. The Pentathlon is not a hierarchical system of priorities; neither is the Old Testament concept of life. Nor does the Pentathlon pit our love for God against our day-to-day responsibilities at work and in the community; neither does the Old Testament model for life.

In short, the Pentathlon helps us look at our responsibilities as God's people in the same comprehensive way that the Old Testament Hebrews were to look at theirs.

Not that we're to be Old Testament people. No, we're to live under the New Covenant brought about by Christ. But the nature of our day-to-day lives and our need to live the entirety of our lives under God's direction has not changed. Let's turn, then, to the New Testament's concept of life.

THE NEW TESTAMENT

When we consider the New Testament, we find that some things have changed radically since Christ, while other things haven't changed at all. One thing that has not changed is the emphasis on holiness in all things, for example, in 1 Peter 1:15-16: "But like the Holy One who called you, be holy yourselves also in all your behavior; because it is written, 'You shall be holy, for I am holy.'"

Does that mean we're to observe dietary restrictions and perform animal sacrifices and carry out the other requirements of the Law? No, because one of the main things that changed with Christ's work on the cross was the need for those ritualistic requirements. In a sense, Christ did away with the special category of "holy" activities by extending the concept of "holiness" to *all* aspects of life. Whatever we do in life is to be done "in the name of the Lord Jesus," that is, with an eye toward His lordship and holiness.

This comprehensive view fits with the way people live, because both before and after Christ, people had jobs to do, marriages to nurture, children to raise, and governments to contend with. And as in the Old Testament, New Testament believers are to relate every facet of their complex lives to God.

We see this clearly in the book of 1 Peter. After exhorting his readers to holiness early in the book, Peter shows the implications of this for everyday behavior. He begins with a summary statement in 1 Peter 2:11-12. Then he addresses himself to the implications in regard to government and the community (2:13-17); work (2:18-25); and the home (3:1-7). Later in the book he treats relationships among believers (4:7-11, 5:1-5). That's a comprehensive view of life!

Now we're very close to something like the Pentathlon. As we examine the New Testament epistles, certain categories of life recur again and again as areas for Christian growth and action: one's personal and spiritual life, family, work, church, and community.

These five seem especially prominent in Paul's letters to the Romans, Ephesians, and Colossians, though they appear throughout the other New Testament books as well. Here's a chart of the particular passages:

	Personal Life	Family	Work	Church	Community
Romans	12:1-2			12:3-21 14:1-23	13:1-14
Ephesians	4:17–5:21 6:10-20	5:22–6:4	6:5-12	4:1-16	
Colossians	3:1-17	3:18-21	3:22–4:1		4:5-6

You might want to go through the other epistles and add to this chart. For instance, I've already analyzed 1 Peter. But 1 Thessalonians 4:9-12 and 2 Thessalonians 3:6-15 discuss work. Galatians 5:16-26 is a key passage on personal spirituality. And 1 and 2 Corinthians have major sections dealing with church issues.

The point here is not to cram every verse in the New Testament into a chart. Life is far too complex for that sort of wooden classification. But in presenting the Pentathlon, I'm trying to help us grasp at least three major truths about the New Testament's teaching on life.

The New Testament is realistic about how people live. To hear or read some Christian teachers, you'd think that Christ can work only with someone who drops out of society and becomes weird. But that's silly. Jesus claimed to be the Lord of *all* of life: "All authority has been given to Me in heaven and on earth" (Matthew 28:18).

If that's true, then we should be able to serve Him as Lord in any normal activity of life. If we have to quit our job and quit our community and quit our church and take our family to a deserted island and go away by ourselves on a beach in order for Jesus to become our Lord, something is wrong!

That may be necessary for a few. But for most of us, if Christianity is real and true, it had better work in the world that we all have to face every day. It had better make sense when we're negotiating a lease, preparing a resume, using the copier, calling in sick, answering the phone, describing our boss to a coworker, cashing our paycheck, and in the myriad other aspects of our work life. And it had better make just as much sense when we head home after work, when we go to church, when we interact with our neighbors, and when we sit alone with our private thoughts and feelings.

I believe that biblical Christianity is relevant to every aspect of our lives. It helps us deal with life as it is, not as we might wish it to be. It accepts that your boss may be a jerk. It understands that your husband may not be interested in the Lord. It realizes that governments can make life difficult for people who love God. It is not shocked when you feel angry at God, or forsaken by Him, or disappointed by unanswered prayer.

In fact, the Bible is far more realistic about life than many of those who teach the Bible! That's a good reason to study it first-hand, and not just take someone's word for what it says.

The New Testament is comprehensive in its teaching.
To hear some people talk, you'd think God is interested only in prayer, hymns, and evangelism. But that's such a limited view, both of God and of life.

Fortunately, in the Bible God has shown us what matters to Him. And the fact that the New Testament touches upon every major category of life shows that it *all* matters to Him!

The New Testament shows that Christ is the Lord over all of life.
The integrating point for the New Testament's teaching is Jesus Christ. His lordship—and our relationship

to Him—is the mainspring that drives the entire apparatus.

The questions, then, become: How can we honor Christ as Lord in our day-to-day lives? How can we live out a biblically balanced lifestyle? Practically speaking, how can we put our work back into proper perspective with the other four areas of life? These are questions of strategy, and it's to them we now turn in Part Three.

PART THREE

Putting Work in Its Proper Perspective!

CHAPTER EIGHT

"APPLYing" the Pentathlon

Have you ever given your kids a Christmas present that had to be assembled—only to find that the manufacturer forgot to include the instructions? Bill recalls that one year his folks bought his brother a beautiful German-made bike. On Christmas Eve his dad sneaked the package home and pulled it out of the car once the children were in bed.

Opening the box, however, his parents were dismayed to find that while the instructions were included, they were in German! For a while they struggled to make sense of the document, using a tattered German-English dictionary. But finally, in frustration, they tossed the paper aside and trusted common sense to bolt the machine together. Granted, they ended up with a few spare parts, but on the whole the bike operated just fine.

Well, having offered the Pentathlon as a model for New Testament living, I don't want to be guilty of stopping here with the label, "User Assembly Required." That would be foolish. Many of us already feel that the instructions we hear for how to live the Christian life might as well be in German—or Greek and Hebrew! That's why I want to describe some very practical strategies for using the Pentathlon in day-to-day life.

However, as we turn to the nuts and bolts of balancing competing time demands, I'm assuming two things. First, that you've covered the discussion in Parts One and Two of this book, particularly the material on the Pentathlon in Chapter 6. If not, I strongly urge you to do so. Without that foundation, the ideas and suggestions that follow may seem arbitrary and superficial.

I'm also assuming, of course, that you agree with the concept of the Pentathlon as a biblical model for planning, and that you've read this far because your sincere desire is to faithfully please God with the many resources and responsibilities He's given you.

How can you do that? How can you use the Pentathlon in your life to achieve biblical balance? Let me suggest one strategy that I and many others have found to be very helpful. An easy way to summarize it is to remember the acronym "A-P-P-L-Y."

A-P-P-L-Y

A-P-P-L-Y stands for five stages or steps you'll need to go through as part of an intentional, planned process of growth. Here's what each letter stands for and means:

A stands for "Analyze the Scriptures."
If you want your life to reflect biblical values, you must first understand what those biblical values are. And there's only one way to do that—*analyze* what the Bible says about each of the five categories of life.

In Chapter 9, I'll mention a dozen or so principles from Scripture for each area of the Pentathlon. (There are hundreds more.) The point is that you begin with God's Word as your foundation for a balanced lifestyle.

P stands for "Personal Inventory."

One of the great points of breakdown for people when they talk about applying God's Word is that they often neglect to evaluate where they stand in relation to the truth presented.

For instance, Ephesians 4:25 tells us to "speak truth." No one would question the rightness of that. Yet I know people who would champion that biblical ideal, yet would think nothing of inflating their academic and career achievements on a resume! That's because they've never taken a *personal inventory* of how well they are applying God's truth in practical ways in each of the five areas.

In Chapter 10, I'll let you take such an inventory. The purpose is not to point out all the things you may be failing at in your life. Rather, I want to help you discover practical areas in which you can grow more toward Christlikeness.

P stands for "Plan Steps."

After you've analyzed God's Word and taken a personal inventory of how your life corresponds to it, it's time to plan steps to devise practical strategies for growth. This is really a process of goal setting.

The term "goal setting" is a problem for many. Some people get confused over what a goal is. Others don't like the concept. It sounds too contrived to them, too legalistic, too confining. And others have a hard time translating biblical principles into specific action steps that they can take.

So I'll examine the process of goal setting in Chapter

11. I think you'll find that planning practical steps for Christian growth is a simple, natural activity. Far from being confining, it's a liberating exercise that brings specificity and direction to the growth process.

L stands for "Liability."
What I have in mind here is setting up a support system of peers who will encourage you as you take the action steps you've planned. Some people call this "accountability," though that's another loaded term that will require discussion. But the point is, you'll find it easier to follow through on your commitments if you have someone to whom you hold yourself liable.

In Chapter 12, I'll show you how to ally yourself with a supportive group of your associates. For many people, this resource has become the most valuable asset they've gleaned from this study. A common comment I've heard is, "You've helped me find my first friends!"

Y stands for "Yardstick."
The only way you'll really continue to grow and to use the Pentathlon model is if you can measure your progress. To do that, you'll need a yardstick, some means of evaluating whether you're getting anywhere.

In Chapter 13, I'll suggest evaluation strategies, such as a checklist and a journal. Using tools like these, or others that you design, you'll find that over time you're making noticeable progress in balancing your life and growing toward Christlikeness.

WILL IT WORK?

Sometimes when I've laid out the A-P-P-L-Y strategy, I've found that some people expect too much from it, while others expect too little. Those who expect too much usually think that I've devised a foolproof way to end up at Christian maturity in five easy steps. I assure you, no such process exists.

The five stages of the A-P-P-L-Y method are my best attempt at breaking down the process of growth so that we can manage it in bite-sized pieces. It looks neat and clean on paper, but in reality, the process is usually a two-steps-forward, one-step-back sort of journey. It's a lot messier than we'd like.

This may be disconcerting to you if you like structure and predictability, but don't get too discouraged. Go ahead and use the A-P-P-L-Y grid. I think you'll find it helpful. While it can't change the unpredictable nature of life, it can provide a framework for your progress. And some structure is better than none at all.

"Oh, yeah?!" cries another handful of people, who can't stand anything that's rigid and "canned." They see a stratagem like the A-P-P-L-Y method as wooden, authoritarian, and contrived. They are skeptical as to whether such a system will work. Instead, they prefer a more freestyle approach.

This is probably just a matter of personality and taste. A-P-P-L-Y may not suit everyone. If it doesn't feel right to you or fit with your way of getting things done, perhaps you can devise a strategy of your own that's more effective for you.

However, be sure that in saying no to the A-P-P-L-Y model you're not falling into one of the six fallacies of Christian growth mentioned in Chapter 4, especially the wishin'-and-hopin' fallacy. Christian growth doesn't automatically happen. So even if the A-P-P-L-Y concept doesn't work for you, be sure to find a strategy that will.

The test of whether any plan of growth is effective is

whether it produces measurable, tangible change in two key areas: your character and your behavior. No strategy, not even A-P-P-L-Y, is of much use unless it's changing the way you think, your attitudes and values, and unless it makes a difference in your actions and choices. The goal, remember, is Christlikeness. Are we becoming more like Him?

IS A-P-P-L-Y BIBLICAL?

Some people object to the A-P-P-L-Y scheme because they're not sure it's found in Scripture. "If this is really the way we're supposed to grow as Christians," they'll argue, "then why isn't there a passage in the Bible that lays it out that way?"

My first response is that I'm not so sure it *isn't* found in the Bible. Ephesians 5:15-17 says:

> Therefore be careful how you walk, not as unwise men, but as wise, making the most of your time, because the days are evil. So then do not be foolish, but understand what the will of the Lord is.

"Be careful how you walk," Paul says. That is, take care what you do with your life. Clearly, he has our use of time in view in this passage. And this means that somewhere, the will of God (as expressed in Scripture) has to intersect with our schedule.

Granted, we can't find an acronym in the Bible like A-P-P-L-Y. I think that's because there is not one divinely authorized growth plan that will fit all people in all cultures at all times. If there were, I feel certain that the Holy Spirit would have given it to us.

But when it comes to applying the Word to our lives,

we do find the basic principle that we *must trust God and take steps*. The A-P-P-L-Y device is simply my attempt to explain how we do that in practical terms. Furthermore, I find strong biblical precedent for each element of the A-P-P-L-Y process. So even if it's not explicitly stated, it's certainly implicit in the Bible.

The A-P-P-L-Y method has been extremely helpful to hundreds of people I'm working with. It gives them a structure and some direction that is very encouraging. In fact, I find that most of us want a process that is fairly well-defined and practical. We're tired of Christian "growth" that is nebulous and theoretical. We've tried to practice many of the standard religious platitudes and found that it's like trying to nail Jello to the wall!

In the face of such frustration, the A-P-P-L-Y strategy provides a more solid footing. If you'll work your way through the next few chapters with me, I think you'll agree.

A: Analyze the Scriptures

Imagine working without a job description. I don't mean a job where you're told to "write your own job description." I mean a job *without* a description, where you have no idea why you're there or what you're supposed to do. You'd feel pretty hesitant about doing anything, because without a clear statement of the expectations, you'd always worry that you'd be doing the wrong thing. And you'd feel pretty frustrated, because you'd never know whether you were succeeding or whether you were doing the right thing.

A lot of Christians feel that God has signed them up for some important task, but has failed to provide an adequate job description. That's sad, because in reality, God has clearly spelled out in the Bible what His desires and intentions are for the various categories of life. That's why we begin by analyzing the Scriptures.

But let's be certain of what we mean when we talk about "God's desires and intentions" as revealed in the Bible—what we commonly refer to as "God's will." Some people act as though there is a one-to-one correspondence between verses in the Bible and situations in life. So when you confront a particular circumstance or problem, just plug in the appropriate verse!

Unfortunately, things aren't quite that simple. In the first place, both the Old and New Testaments were written in the context of cultures that differ vastly from ours. So to make the Bible practical to us today, we not only have to translate Hebrew and Greek words into English, but also *translate cultures* as well.

We do that primarily by looking for biblical *principles*. By principles I mean basic truths that the text either clearly or strongly implies. In the material that follows, I'll present some principles for godly living, along with passages that I believe teach those principles.

Take time to read carefully each scriptural passage and consider what it says about God's objectives for *your* life. For each of the five categories of the Pentathlon, there are scores if not hundreds of principles throughout the Bible. I've merely selected a few here to illustrate the process of analyzing the Scriptures. You can continue this kind of analysis on a regular basis on your own.

PERSONAL LIFE

1. You are to cultivate an abiding loyalty and deep commitment to love God with every part of your being.
   Matthew 22:36-38: *"Teacher, which is the great commandment in the Law?" And He said to him, " 'You shall love the LORD your God with all your heart, and with all your soul, and with all your mind.' This is the great and foremost commandment."*
2. You are to cultivate an intimate relationship with Jesus Christ.

Philippians 3:8-10: *I count all things to be loss in view of the surpassing value of knowing Christ Jesus my Lord, for whom I have suffered the loss of all things, and count them but rubbish in order that I may gain Christ, and may be found in Him, not having a righteousness of my own derived from the Law, but that which is through faith in Christ, the righteousness which comes from God on the basis of faith, that I may know Him, and the power of His resurrection and the fellowship of His sufferings, being conformed to His death.*

3. You are to maintain a growing dependence on God.
   Hebrews 11:6: *And without faith it is impossible to please Him, for he who comes to God must believe that He is, and that He is a rewarder of those who seek Him.*

4. You are to serve God with deep gratitude and loyalty in every area of life.
   2 Corinthians 5:14-15: *For the love of Christ controls us, having concluded this, that one died for all, therefore all died; and He died for all, that they who live should no longer live for themselves, but for Him who died and rose again on their behalf.*

5. You are to seek daily spiritual renewal.
   Romans 12:2: *And do not be conformed to this world, but be transformed by the renewing of your mind, that you may prove what the will of God is, that which is good and acceptable and perfect.*

6. You are to exercise self-control and discipline.
   1 Corinthians 9:25-27: *Everyone who competes in the games exercises self-control in all things. They then do it to receive a perishable wreath, but we an imperishable. Therefore I run in such a way, as not without aim; I box in such a way, as not beating the air; but I buffet my body and make it my slave, lest possibly, after I have preached to others, I myself should be disqualified.*

7. You are to cultivate and enjoy friends.
   Proverbs 17:17: *A friend loves at all times, and a
   brother is born for adversity.*
8. You should get adequate rest and leisure.
   Psalm 127:2: *It is vain for you to rise up early,
   to retire late, to eat the bread of painful labors; for He
   gives to His beloved even in his sleep.*
9. You are to cultivate Christlikeness in your character.
   Philippians 2:5-7: *Have this attitude in yourselves
   which was also in Christ Jesus, who, although He
   existed in the form of God, did not regard equality with
   God a thing to be grasped, but emptied Himself, taking
   the form of a bond-servant, and being made in the
   likeness of men.*
10. You are to practice the loyalty and lifestyle of a
    disciple.
    Luke 14:26-27: *"If anyone comes to Me, and does not
    hate his own father and mother and wife and children
    and brothers and sisters, yes, and even his own life, he
    cannot be My disciple. Whoever does not carry his own
    cross and come after Me cannot be My disciple."*
    Luke 14:33: *"So therefore, no one of you can be My
    disciple who does not give up all his own possessions."*
    John 13:34-35: *"A new commandment I give to you,
    that you love one another, even as I have loved you, that
    you also love one another. By this all men will know that
    you are My disciples, if you have love for one another."*
    John 15:8: *"By this is My Father glorified, that you
    bear much fruit, and so prove to be My disciples."*

FAMILY LIFE

1. You are to see yourself as a servant to each member
   of your family, whether or not they are believers.

Mark 10:45: *"For even the Son of Man did not come to be served, but to serve, and to give His life a ransom for many."*

2. Husbands are to provide the proper environment for their wives to grow spiritually.

Ephesians 5:25-26: *Husbands, love your wives, just as Christ also loved the church and gave Himself up for her; that He might sanctify her, having cleansed her by the washing of water with the word.*

3. Husbands are to treat their wives with respect and care.

1 Peter 3:7: *You husbands likewise, live with your wives in an understanding way, as with a weaker vessel, since she is a woman; and grant her honor as a fellow-heir of the grace of life, so that your prayers may not be hindered.*

4. Wives are to respect and honor their husbands and to lead by example.

1 Peter 3:1-6: *In the same way, you wives, be submissive to your own husbands so that even if any of them are disobedient to the word they may be won without a word by the behavior of their wives, as they observe your chaste and respectful behavior. And let not your adornment be external only—braiding the hair, and wearing gold jewelry, and putting on dresses; but let it be the hidden person of the heart, with the imperishable quality of a gentle and quiet spirit, which is precious in the sight of God. For in this way in former times the holy women also, who hoped in God, used to adorn themselves, being submissive to their own husbands. Thus Sarah obeyed Abraham, calling him lord, and you have become her children if you do what is right without being frightened by any fear.*

5. Husbands and wives are to manifest an intimate

union with each other.
Mark 10:7-8: *For this cause a man shall leave his father and mother, and the two shall become one flesh; consequently they are no longer two, but one flesh.*

6. Husbands and wives are to engage in sex with each other.
1 Corinthians 7:3-5: *Let the husband fulfill his duty to his wife, and likewise also the wife to her husband. The wife does not have authority over her own body, but the husband does; and likewise also the husband does not have authority over his own body, but the wife does. Stop depriving one another, except by agreement for a time that you may devote yourselves to prayer, and come together again lest Satan tempt you because of your lack of self-control.*

7. Parents are to provide biblical instruction and wisdom for their children.
Deuteronomy 6:6-7: *"And these words, which I am commanding you today, shall be on your heart; and you shall teach them diligently to your sons and shall talk of them when you sit in your house and when you walk by the way and when you lie down and when you rise up."*

8. Parents are to provide a loving environment for their children.
Proverbs 22:6: *Train up a child in the way he should go, Even when he is old he will not depart from it.*
Ephesians 6:4: *And, fathers, do not provoke your children to anger; but bring them up in the discipline and instruction of the Lord.*

9. Children are to honor their parents.
Ephesians 6:2-3: *Honor your father and mother (which is the first commandment with a promise), that it may be well with you, and that you may live long on the earth.*

10. Parents (fathers especially) are to provide for the

material needs of the family.

1 Timothy 5:8: *But if any one does not provide for his own, and especially for those of his household, he has denied the faith, and is worse than an unbeliever.*

WORK LIFE

1. You are to see yourself as a servant to coworkers and customers.
   Mark 10:45: *"For even the Son of Man did not come to be served, but to serve, and to give His life a ransom for many."*

2. You are to work with a motive of serving Christ, not just people. Your work is an act of worship.
   Ephesians 6:5-7: *Slaves, be obedient to those who are your masters according to the flesh, with fear and trembling, in the sincerity of your heart, as to Christ; not by way of eyeservice, as men-pleasers, but as slaves of Christ, doing the will of God from the heart. With good will render service, as to the Lord, and not to men.*

3. You are to have a healthy balance of work and leisure, not being lazy and not being a workaholic.
   Ecclesiastes 4:5-6: *The fool folds his hands and consumes his own flesh. One hand full of rest is better than two fists full of labor and striving after wind.*

4. You are to mark your work with excellence of effort.
   Colossians 3:23: *Whatever you do, do your work heartily, as for the Lord rather than for men.*

5. You are to maintain a high level of ethical distinction in your attitudes and actions on the job. Your character, your values, and your attitude should be so unique, so Christlike, that coworkers would want to know why.

Philippians 2:15-16: *That you may prove yourselves to be blameless and innocent, children of God above reproach in the midst of a crooked and perverse generation, among whom you appear as lights in the world, holding fast the word of life, so that in the day of Christ I may have cause to glory because I did not run in vain nor toil in vain.*

6. You are to share the gospel with coworkers.
   Mark 16:15: *And He said to them, "Go into all the world and preach the gospel to all creation."*

7. You are to pursue peaceful relationships with coworkers as much as possible, without violating your integrity.
   Romans 12:18: *If possible, so far as it depends on you, be at peace with all men.*
   Hebrews 12:14: *Pursue after peace with all men, and after the sanctification without which no one will see the Lord.*

8. You are to cultivate a sense of gratitude and fulfillment in your work as a gift from God to bring glory to Him.
   Ecclesiastes 3:12-13: *I know that there is nothing better for them than to rejoice and to do good in one's lifetime, moreover, that every man who eats and drinks sees good in all his labor—it is the gift of God.*

9. You are to find contentment in the material blessings you have and not be craving more and more.
   1 Timothy 6:8-10: *And if we have food and covering, with these we shall be content. But those who want to get rich fall into temptation and a snare and many foolish and harmful desires which plunge men into ruin and destruction. For the love of money is a root of all sorts of evil, and some by longing for it have wandered away from the faith, and pierced themselves*

with many a pang.

10. You are to submit to your boss and to the rules of your company, with a good attitude.

Titus 2:9-10: *Urge bondslaves to be subject to their own masters in everything, to be well pleasing, not argumentative, not pilfering, but showing all good faith that they may adorn the doctrine of God our Savior in every respect.*

1 Peter 2:18: *Servants, be submissive to your masters with all respect, not only to those who are good and gentle, but also to those who are unreasonable.*

CHURCH LIFE

1. You are to be a servant to other Christians.

Philippians 2:3-4: *Do nothing from selfishness or empty conceit, but with humility of mind let each of you regard one another as more important than himself; do not merely look out for your own personal interests, but also for the interests of others.*

2. You are to maintain regular fellowship and worship with other believers.

Hebrews 10:25: *Not forsaking our own assembling together, as is the habit of some, but encouraging one another; and all the more, as you see the day drawing near.*

3. You are to use your spiritual gift(s).

Romans 12:6-8: *And since we have gifts that differ according to the grace given to us, let each exercise them accordingly: if prophecy, according to the proportion of his faith; if service, in his serving; or he who teaches, in his teaching; or he who exhorts, in his exhortation; he who gives, with liberality; he who leads, with diligence; he who shows mercy, with cheerfulness.*

4. You are to help those in need.

   1 John 3:17: *But whoever has the world's goods, and beholds his brother in need and closes his heart against him, how does the love of God abide in him?*

5. You are to honor and remain loyal to other Christians.

   Romans 12:10: *Be devoted to one another in brotherly love; give preference to one another in honor.*

6. You are to encourage and build up other Christians.

   1 Thessalonians 5:11: *Therefore encourage one another, and build up one another, just as you also are doing.*

   Hebrews 10:24: *And let us consider how to stimulate one another to love and good deeds.*

7. You are to support financially those whose primary occupation is the proclamation and application of the gospel.

   1 Corinthians 9:14: *So also the Lord directed those who proclaim the gospel to get their living from the gospel.*

8. You are to maintain regular fellowship and Bible study.

   Acts 2:42: *And they were continually devoting themselves to the apostles' teaching and to fellowship, to the breaking of bread and to prayer.*

9. You are to accept other Christians for who they are.

   Romans 15:7: *Wherefore, accept one another, just as Christ also accepted us to the glory of God.*

10. Older women are to teach and set an example for younger women.

    Titus 2:3-4: *Older women likewise are to be reverent in their behavior, not malicious gossips, nor enslaved to much wine, teaching what is good, that they may encourage the young women to love their husbands, to love their children.*

COMMUNITY LIFE

1. You are to see yourself as a servant to nonChristians in your community and in the world.
   Galatians 6:10 (NIV): *Therefore, as we have opportunity, let us do good to all people.*
2. You are to proclaim Christ by your life and words.
   Mark 16:15: *And He said to them, "Go into all the world and preach the gospel to all creation."*
   Philippians 2:14-15: *Do all things without grumbling or disputing; that you may prove yourselves to be blameless and innocent, children of God above reproach in the midst of a crooked and perverse generation, among whom you appear as lights in the world.*
3. You are to pursue the moral health of your culture.
   Matthew 5:16: *"Let your light shine before men in such a way that they may see your good works, and glorify your Father who is in heaven."*
   1 Timothy 2:1-4 (NIV): *I urge, then, first of all, that requests, prayers, intercession and thanksgiving be made for everyone—for kings and all those in authority, that we may live peaceful and quiet lives in all godliness and holiness. This is good, and pleases God our Savior, who wants all men to be saved and to come to a knowledge of the truth.*
4. You are to help the poor.
   Galatians 2:10: *They only asked us to remember the poor—the very thing I also was eager to do.*
5. You are to seek to preserve and protect God's creation.
   Genesis 2:15: *Then the LORD God took the man and put him into the garden of Eden to cultivate it and keep it.*
6. You are to be an example of good works and maintain a good reputation with unbelievers.

1 Timothy 3:7: *And he must have a good reputation with those outside the church, so that he may not fall into reproach and the snare of the devil.*

1 Peter 2:12 (NIV): *Live such good lives among the pagans that, though they accuse you of doing wrong, they may see your good deeds and glorify God on the day he visits us.*

7. You should know how to explain the gospel of Jesus Christ to someone else, and tell why you are a follower of Christ.

   1 Peter 3:15 (NIV): *Always be prepared to give an answer to everyone who asks you to give the reason for the hope that you have.*

8. You are to obey the law and those in authority.

   1 Peter 2:13-14: *Submit yourselves for the Lord's sake to every human institution: whether to a king as the one in authority; or to governors as sent by him for the punishment of evildoers and the praise of those who do right.*

9. You are to pay your taxes.

   Romans 13:7: *Render to all what is due them: tax to whom tax is due; custom to whom custom; fear to whom fear; honor to whom honor.*

10. To the extent you can, you are to avoid being a financial burden on society.

    1 Thessalonians 4:11-12: *Make it your ambition to lead a quiet life and attend to your own business and work with your hands, just as we commanded you; so that you may behave properly toward outsiders and not be in any need.*

CONCLUSION

You may be feeling a bit overwhelmed after reading through these various expectations. Especially when you realize that I've only scratched the surface of the many principles for godly living contained in Scripture.

In fact, you may be more than overwhelmed—you may feel defeated. Especially if you know that you're failing in many or perhaps even most of these areas. If so, let me encourage you with an important truth from Psalm 103:8,10,13-14:

> The LORD is compassionate and gracious,
> Slow to anger and abounding in lovingkind-
> ness. . . .
> He has not dealt with us according to our sins,
> Nor rewarded us according to our iniquities . . .
> Just as a father has compassion on his children,
> So the LORD has compassion on those who fear
> Him.
> For He Himself knows our frame;
> He is mindful that we are but dust.

There are so many more principles, taught not only explicitly in passages like those mentioned, but also implicitly in the many stories, poems, and biographical sketches in Scripture. I encourage you to read and study your Bible daily, looking for principles that you can apply in your life.

That's really the point of Bible study—that you'll live differently as a result. After all, God didn't write the Bible to have it studied; He wrote it to change lives. In God's eyes, the priority is not knowledge, but *obedience*.

To what extent do you obey God? The personal inventory in the next chapter will help you answer that question by letting you evaluate yourself in some specific ways.

CHAPTER TEN

P: Take a Personal Inventory

Once we've analyzed the Scriptures to ferret out principles for godly living, we then have to ask ourselves this question: "How are we doing in light of what God's Word says?" This is an important question, because we want to avoid the fallacy of knowing what God says, but failing to apply it to our lives. In fact, this is what the Apostle James specifically warned against in his epistle:

> But prove yourselves doers of the word, and not merely hearers who delude themselves. For if any one is a hearer of the word and not a doer, he is like a man who looks at his natural face in a mirror; for once he has looked at himself and gone away, he has immediately forgotten what kind of person he was. But one who looks intently at the perfect law, the law of liberty and abiaes by it, not having become a forgetful hearer but an effectual doer, this man shall be blessed in what he does. (James 1:22-25)

When I get out of bed in the morning, before I go to work, I always look at myself in the mirror to see what needs fixing. That invariably leads to a shave, a combing of the hair, and an adjustment of my tie.

Now suppose I saw that I needed all that but just headed out the door without a shave, without combing my hair, and without straightening my tie. If you were my first appointment, you'd probably remark, "Doug! You look like you slept in the gutter! What happened?"

I'm afraid that many Christians are walking around today looking ragged and disheveled, when they should look better! What's the problem? I think it's that although they've studied God's Word, they haven't really evaluated their true condition in the light of the Word. As James says, they've looked in the mirror and then walked away, forgetting to adjust their lives in accordance with God's will.

I want to help you avoid that sort of superficial Christianity. And to do that, I've devised a brief personal inventory, a review of some specific behaviors that characterize mature believers.

TWO CAUTIONS

You may find the idea of answering an inventory to be rather intimidating. That's normal. In fact, even though Bill and I put together the inventory below, we find ourselves uncomfortable whenever we go through it. Why? Because no one likes to see their failures put on paper in front of them. It's embarrassing!

However, the point of this exercise is not to embarrass you or make you feel guilty. Rather, it's intended to point out specific areas in which you could grow more toward Christlikeness. So take this inventory in the spirit in which it's given.

A second caution has to do with the nature of the questions asked on the inventory. You'll notice that they are *very* specific—far more specific even than the principles presented in Chapter 9. In general, the inventory examines specific behaviors rather than general attitudes and actions.

That's because if I ask you to evaluate yourself in light of a general principle, you'll tend to say that you were following that principle quite well, whether you are or not. Not that you'd necessarily lie, but you'd tend to give yourself the benefit of the doubt. Most people would. It's just human nature.

But if I ask you to tell me, yes or no, whether you're behaving in a specific way, you'll tend to give an answer that is much closer to the truth. That's why the inventory asks about specific behaviors that flow out of biblical principles. We want you to be as specific as you can about yourself.

But, again, remember that God is gracious. He accepts you where you are, with all your weaknesses and deficiencies. He also sees you clearly and wants you to see yourself clearly. So don't get overwhelmed. Instead, allow this survey to excite you with the potential for growth and progress.

Realize, of course, that this is by no means a scientific survey. It's just a quick review of some categories. We could have asked a thousand other questions, but these are enough to get a general sketch of where your life is in relation to God's Word.

Taking the inventory is simple: just circle *yes* or *no* in response to each question. Don't spend too much time trying to decide between the two. Usually, the first answer that comes to your mind is the most accurate.

PERSONAL LIFE

1. Do you have a daily time of reading the Bible?   Yes   No
2. Have you read completely through the Bible?   Yes   No
3. Do you have a regular Bible study or discipleship group with whom you meet?   Yes   No
4. Do you have a daily time of prayer?   Yes   No
When and for how long? _____
5. Do you have a prayer plan to pray for people?   Yes   No
6. Do you regularly meet with a friend socially?   Yes   No
7. Do you plan regular periods of rest and recreation on a weekly, monthly, and annual basis?   Yes   No
8. Do you consider yourself overweight?   Yes   No
9. Do you feel you should get more exercise?   Yes   No
10. Do you regularly discuss your needs and problems, thoughts and feelings with your spouse and/or a close friend?   Yes   No

FAMILY

1. Do you and your spouse "date" regularly?   Yes   No
2. Do you regularly have family devotions?   Yes   No
3. Do you regularly take time to talk with your spouse about anything that matters to either of you?   Yes   No

4. Do you regularly spend individual time
   with each of your children, giving
   them focused attention?   Yes   No
   When and how long? _____
5. Would your family rate you as physically affectionate?   Yes   No
6. Does your family plan family fun and
   togetherness each week?   Yes   No
7. Wives, would your husband say you
   follow his leadership?   Yes   No
8. Husbands, would your wife say you are
   a good leader?   Yes   No
9. If your parents are still living, do you
   call or visit them regularly to see what
   their needs are?   Yes   No
10. Do you have a budget to control your
    family finances?   Yes   No
    Where is it? _____
11. Do you and your spouse have a weekly
    time of planning?   Yes   No

WORK

1. Do you regularly plan out your day and
   set priorities?   Yes   No
2. Do you routinely pray for coworkers?   Yes   No
   When? _____
3. Could you give a clear presentation of
   the gospel to a nonChristian coworker?   Yes   No
4. Can you point to one area of your job
   in which you've improved in the past
   year?   Yes   No
   What is it? _____
5. Do you stay current with changes and

developments in your profession? Yes No

6. Is there any area of ethical compromise in your work? Yes No
What is it? _____

7. Are you clear on how your job helps others? Yes No

8. Do you tend to work too many hours? Yes No

9. Do you worry excessively about your work? Yes No

10. Do you find that problems at your work cause significant frustration and anger when you come home? Yes No

CHURCH

1. Do you know what your spiritual gift is? Yes No

2. Do you talk with and affirm your pastor? Yes No

3. Do you have a regular program of giving to those who proclaim the gospel? Yes No

4. Do you have regular fellowship with others who will challenge you spiritually? Yes No

5. Do you regularly call or write other Christians to thank them for something they've done or to encourage them in their faith? Yes No

6. Do you routinely pray for other Christians? Yes No
When and for how long? _____

7. Do you ever practice hospitality to Christians in need? Yes No

8. Do you have anyone who holds you

accountable to reach personal goals? Yes No

9. Do you have any direct contact with
   missionaries? Yes No
   Who? _____

10. Are you involved in any form of
    financial assistance to those in need? Yes No

COMMUNITY

1. Do you regularly meet socially with
   nonChristians? Yes No

2. Do you have any close nonChristian
   friends? Yes No

3. Do nonChristians feel comfortable
   around you? Yes No

4. Do you know your neighbors? Yes No

5. Can you give a clear, concise presentation of the gospel? Yes No

6. Do you regularly pray for government
   leaders and other officials? Yes No

7. Are you involved in any community
   service projects? Yes No
   Which ones? _____

8. Are you giving money to feed the poor? Yes No

9. Are you aware of the political issues in
   your area? Yes No

10. Have you shared the gospel with some-
    one in the last six months? Yes No
    To whom? _____

MAKING THE MOST OF THIS INVENTORY

Having completed this personal inventory, you're almost
ready to start planning some specific action steps for

growth. To prepare for that, look back over your responses. If you've been honest, you'll probably find some areas in which you're excelling and some in which you could improve. You'll also tend to find that you're doing better in one or two of the categories, say work or home, than in the others.

As you look over the list, start thinking about ways you'd like to grow, ways in which you'd like to change and become more Christlike. See if you can narrow down one or two items in each category. In fact, I suggest you stop right now and pray, thanking God for the victories on the list, and asking Him to put His finger on issues that are especially problematic for you.

Once you've isolated five or ten such items, you're ready to move on to the next chapter, where we'll look at the important process of goal setting.

CHAPTER ELEVEN

P: Plan Steps

It never ceases to amaze me how carefully people plan their work—and how much they achieve as a result. Think of the planning and strategy that went into putting a man on the moon. Or the masterful job of organization that made the Olympics in Los Angeles such a success. Or the painstaking sketch work that preceded each of Leonardo da Vinci's masterpieces.

Such achievements illustrate that forethought tends toward excellence, while negligence leaves everything up to chance. This is true in both work and nonwork areas. To be sure, plans don't always work out as we expect. And sometimes God "bails us out" despite poor planning. But the fact remains that without direction, most of us will just wander around, without purpose and without growth.

Yet while planning is demanded in the workplace, it's often abandoned once we're off the job. As the saying goes, we don't plan to fail—we fail to plan! Is it any wonder, then, if we struggle in our growth as people? As another saying observes, if we aim at nothing, we'll hit it every time. However, as I mentioned in an earlier chapter, goal setting is something of a red flag to some. Perhaps the place to begin, then, is by defining our terms.

WHAT IS A GOAL?

Sometimes when I talk with people about setting goals for Christian growth, I discover that what I mean by a goal is different from their understanding of a goal. In fact, there seems to be a whole class of words that gets thrown about only to confuse the issue: *goals, objectives, plans, strategy, intention, steps, purpose,* and *mission*. To make matters worse, I haven't found these words used uniformly in the business community.

In this chapter when I talk about a *goal*, I mean a specific action or behavior that you intend to take in order to grow toward Christlikeness. As we look at sample goals, you'll quickly understand what I mean.

SETTING GOALS

If you intend to put your work in proper perspective and if you intend to faithfully please God with the resources and responsibilities He's given you, it's imperative that you go beyond good intentions and *plan steps* for accomplishing those good intentions. Sooner or later, good intentions must lead to activity.

Say, for instance, that you're a husband and you've been reading Peter's first letter. You've come across verse 7 in chapter 3, which outlines your responsibilities toward your wife, and you see the reason given: "So that your prayers may not be hindered." You begin to reflect on this curious phrase, and it occurs to you that it's a biblical principle for husbands and wives to pray together. You also know that you and your wife don't do that. On the basis of this passage, you feel you should.

Up to this point, it's only a good intention. How can you start praying together?

When it comes to setting goals, I've found a little acronym to be helpful: S-M-A-C. As you set goals, you'll want to make them *specific, measurable, achievable,* and *compatible.*

S—Specific

The fatal flaw of most goals is that they are too general. The more specific you can make your goals, the better.

> •*"I'm going to start praying with my wife."*
> Poor! Too vague; it'll never happen; it's still only a good intention.
> •*"I'm going to discuss with my wife how we can start praying together more."*
> Better! Still a bit vague, though.
> •*"I'm going to see if my wife will pray with me tomorrow."*
> Good! Now we're starting to get more specific. But there's still room for improvement.
> •*"I'm going to try and pray with my wife for five minutes before bed once before the end of this week."*
> Superb! Extremely specific and practical.

M—Measurable

Another flaw in many goals is that you can never tell whether or not you've achieved them. They're not only not specific; they're not measurable. What you want is a statement that you can determine whether or not it's been achieved with a simple yes or no.

•*"I'm going to spend more time with my daughter."*
Poor! Not only vague, but what does "more time"
mean?
•*"I'm going to spend Saturday morning playing with
my daughter."*
Better! But at what point Saturday will you be able
to say you've accomplished your goal?
•*"I'm going to help my daughter learn to ride her new
bike this Saturday morning right after breakfast."*
Very good! Both you and your daughter, or anyone
else, would be able to tell me at noon on Saturday
whether you've done this.

A—Achievable

Often goals don't happen because they're hopelessly
unrealistic. I find that when it comes to goals, less is
usually more! That is, if we'll bite off less at a time, we'll
actually accomplish more over a period of time. Consequently, we need to build realism into our goals.

For example, Fred's family finances are a disaster.
He doesn't know much about where the money is coming from, and he certainly doesn't know where it is
going. He doesn't know how much debt he has, nor what
his spending priorities should be, nor what his future
financial needs are likely to be. Here are some possible
goals that Fred might set:

•*"I'm going to get my finances straightened out."*
Poor! Fred's standing on the Titanic telling me he
thinks it's about time he learned to swim!
•*"I'm going to sit down next Saturday and set up a
budget."*
Better! At least Fred's getting specific. But I still
don't know whether he has any idea what he's

doing. How can he set up a budget until he knows where the money's going?

• *"Saturday morning I'm going to get all my bank statements out and balance my checkbook."*

Great! This is a good place to start. This goal is specific and measurable. It's also achievable. If Fred reconciles his checkbook with his bank statement this Saturday, he'll be in good shape to start outlining his budget categories at a later time.

C—Compatible

One of the often overlooked aspects of goal setting is that it never happens in a vacuum. You already have plenty of other responsibilities and commitments. If you start adding more, you'll have to adjust your previous routine to fit them in. In other words, your new goals must be compatible with your circumstances.

This follows from something we said in Chapter 6 about the Pentathlon: every area affects every other area. Consequently, as you set goals, you'll need to consider how your intentions will affect the other areas of your life. A good rule of thumb is: whenever you add a responsibility or a commitment to one area, you'll have to subtract something somewhere else.

This is really the nub of balancing competing time demands. What you'll find is that you'll either need to limit your goals, or else you'll need to cut back in other areas of your life in order to accommodate your goals.

For instance, take a goal related to fitness: "I plan to go to my health club three mornings a week between 6:15 and 7:30 for a workout." On the face of it, that sounds like a good goal. It's specific, measurable, and achievable. But is it compatible? That all depends on who is saying it and on the nature of his or her other responsibilities.

That goal might work for some executives. It probably wouldn't for many men who work construction and have to be at the site by 7:00 or 7:30. It might work for a single woman, but definitely not for a working mother. A later time might work for a career homemaker whose children are in school. But it almost certainly would never be compatible with the life of a single parent who has to work.

SOME SAMPLE GOALS

What follows is a selection of sample goals to help you think about the kinds of goals you might want to set for yourself.

Personal Life
1. Read the Bible fifteen minutes a day, five days a week.
2. Pray through my prayer list each day of the week.
3. Meet with others for fellowship weekly.
4. Join a drama club for one season.
5. Meet with friends once a week.
6. Date spouse weekly.
7. Attain weight of _____ by [date].
8. Complete a quilt by [date].
9. Get eight hours of rest each night.
10. Limit myself to one moderate helping of each item per meal with no dessert.

Family
1. Have family devotions three times a week.
2. Reserve one night a week for skits and other

homespun entertainment with the family.
3. Pray together as a family for five minutes each day.
4. Memorize one Bible verse per week as a family.
5. Attend church together weekly.
6. Hug my child three times a day.
7. Date my spouse once a week.
8. Devote one Saturday a month to family fun and togetherness.
9. Say "I love you" to my son once each day.
10. Set up a family budget.

Work Life
1. Invite [name of coworker] over for dinner by [date].
2. Pray for [name], [name], and [name] once a week.
3. Leave the house no later than [time] each morning to get to work on time.
4. Plan lunch with [name of coworker] some day this week to encourage him.
5. Develop a clear business plan to ensure long-term business growth, viability, and stability by [date].
6. Review my employees' salaries to be sure they are fair and equitable.
7. Read one article each week or a book each month that discusses developments in my profession.
8. Review my job description each month.
9. Leave work by [time] each day in order to get home on time.
10. Arrange a meeting with [name of coworker] to try to resolve a conflict we're having.

Church Life
1. Teach a Sunday school class this semester.
2. Lead a Bible study with women in my neighborhood twice a month.

3. Meet with [name] once a week to help him in his growth as a new believer.
4. Invite one couple over after church each week.
5. Express appreciation each week to those who teach me.
6. Give to the following Christian organizations: [List, with amounts].
7. Write a letter each month as a family to a missionary's family.
8. Ask my pastor each month how I can pray for him.
9. Study one hymn a month, both the words and the music, in order to sing it with more insight and conviction.
10. Meet with my child's Sunday school teacher to learn what is being taught.

Community

1. Learn how to share the gospel by attending a training class.
2. Take a course in apologetics by [date].
3. Have one nonChristian couple over each month.
4. Join [name of organization] in order to develop relationships with nonChristians by [date].
5. Lead an evangelistic Bible study with my neighbors, starting [date].
6. Visit a nursing home once a month with my family to encourage an elderly person.
7. Give [amount] a month to an agency working with the poor.
8. Pray for one country of the world each day or week.
9. Get involved in inner-city renewal with [name of organization].
10. Pray for government officials by individual names each week.

NOW IT'S YOUR TURN

It's time for you to formulate some goals of your own. This should be fairly easy if you've completed the personal inventory and evaluated your responses in the ways I suggested at the end of Chapter 10. Select one item from each of the five categories and design a goal to help you grow in that area. Remember what we've said about making your goals *specific, measurable, achievable,* and *compatible*. Write your goals below or in a separate notebook.

Personal _____

Family _____

Work _____

Church _____

Community _____

One last thing: Write these goals into your schedule book or on your calendar where appropriate to help you work them into your schedule.

And then—*do them!*

CHAPTER TWELVE

L: Make Yourself Liable to Others

A young upstart salesman had worked months to close a multi-million-dollar deal. He'd scoped out the prospect, researched the customer's needs, and initiated a series of meetings and luncheons to cultivate interest and pursuade his client to buy the product. Finally, after the eager beaver delivered a smashing close, the prospect, who had been cautious to the extreme, paused and finally nodded. "Okay," he said. "Let's do it. I'll take five units to start. As soon as you deliver them, I'll cut you a check."

The salesman was ecstatic! His commission would be in six-figures! He was so excited with the outcome that he left the meeting bursting with enthusiasm to tell his wife the good news. As he drove home, he decided to get her some flowers. Then he decided he'd take her out for dinner to celebrate, so he used his car phone to reserve a table at the most prestigious club in town.

About this time he began to reflect on what his wife would wear, and it occurred to him that she needed a fur coat. So he stopped at a furrier and purchased a rare, full-length spotted mink with matching hat.

Then he decided to splurge! He visited a mall where he picked out a bottle of perfume, priced at $350 for a half-ounce. She'd love it!

Well, he'd pretty much taken care of his wife, so he turned his thoughts to what he'd like for himself. It didn't take him long to decide. His next stop was at the Porsche dealership, where he took delivery on a jet black 914 with a big spoiler and a customized leather interior with alligator appointments. Was he hot or what?!

Needless to say, he had quite a party for the next few weeks. He bought gifts for all his friends, new toys for his kids. It was as if he'd won the lottery!

But it all came to a screeching halt when his boss called him into the office late one Friday. "Son," he said, "you did a great job on that account. You set things up. You worked the customer in textbook fashion. You even closed the deal at the perfect time. That's why I want you to have this," and he handed the salesman an envelope. Inside was a check for $275!

"What's this?" asked the startled young man.

"Your walking papers!" replied the boss with an icy stare. "You did everything right. But you forgot one *minor* detail—you never sent the man his product!"

Could anyone be so stupid? Would a person campaign for President of the United States, endure the onslaughts of a grueling campaign trail, get elected, only to skip the inauguration?

Would a football team scrap and scrape its way through training camp, endure fifteen weeks of a bone-crunching season, and survive several rounds of playoff games, only to forfeit an appearance at the Super Bowl? Would a starry-eyed groom woo the love of his life, pursuade her to marry him, and pursuade her folks to pay for the wedding, only to be a no-show at the altar?

Of course not! Yet that's exactly what it would be like to set up goals as I've described, and then fail to follow through! That's why I ended the last chapter with a simple exhortation about goals: Do them!

However, I'm realistic enough—some would say, skeptical enough—to know that for the vast majority of people, that's still not enough. In other words, even after all we've been through—even after you've gotten ahold of this book, and even after we've gone through the many reasons why people get work out of perspective, and even after we've laid out the Pentathlon model and explained the A-P-P-L-Y concept, and looked at scriptural objectives and a personal inventory and a process of goal setting with the S-M-A-C principles, and even after you've come up with five goals of your own and put them on your schedule—even after all of that, if you're like most people, you'll have a hard time following through! Especially over the long haul. You may stay with it for a week or a month. But very few people stick with a steady, measured process of growth over a long period of time. You may be the rare exception, but most of us don't have staying power.

Unless, of course, we have some help. I recall, for instance, that in college I was part of the wrestling team. I can remember how we'd prepare for the championship tournaments. Several weeks before the matches, we'd go into an incredibly grueling regimen that was far worse than the two-day tournament itself.

Our practice routine began with warm-up exercises and extensive stretching of muscles and ligaments. Then we would run two miles. Then we'd start our practice matches.

This would mean that the first-string wrestlers,

including me, would get down on the mats and take on the second-string guys. We'd wrestle for nine minutes. Then the third-string would take over for the second-string, and we'd wrestle for another nine minutes. After that, the fourth-string guys would get their turn!

Tired yet? Too bad! We'd go out and run two more miles, and then come back and wrestle for two more matches. Only then would we warm down and head for the locker room.

This exhausting routine went on for nearly two weeks—tearing us down and building us up, again and again. Needless to say, by the time the tournament rolled around, we were in top shape, ready to go.

I don't think I've ever faced a more grueling discipline of physical exercise in my life. And I've often reflected on the factors that kept me going. Obviously the prospect of capturing a championship was a motivating force. But without question, the single greatest element of motivation was the presence of my coach and my teammates. Somehow there was a bond there that kept me and the other guys from slacking off. Call it peer pressure, accountability, whatever. A powerful group dynamic was at play that kept us going, achieving levels of physical strength, endurance, and skill that would have been unimaginable on our own.

The dynamic involved, obviously, is a level of liability before others. There is a unique power to a group of peers who act as a team to ensure each member's success. And if you make use of that powerful group dynamic in your own growth, you'll stand a much better chance of following through on the commitments you make and the goals you set.

Consider some of the many benefits derived from such a group.

ACCOUNTABILITY

I felt a real accountability to my wrestling coach and the other guys on the team. By "accountability" I mean a sense of obligation, of sacrificing my own tendencies to slack off in order to ensure the success of the team.

Many Christians distrust this idea of accountability. Bill recalls an interesting encounter he once had. A prominent Christian musician was coming through town, and Bill had the opportunity to meet this artist's promoter-manager.

You may know that life on the road is very hard for people in music or theater. In fact, it can be extremely damaging to marriages and morals. Knowing this, Bill asked the promoter, "I'm curious to know how you all handle accountability when you're out on the road like this?"

Without a moment's hesitation, the promoter shot back defensively, "What do you mean, 'accountability'? We don't need anyone looking over our shoulders, checking up on us!"

Later they had a chance to sit down and discuss this issue. The promoter explained that he didn't find "accountability" taught in Scripture. Instead, he felt it was the product of an authoritarian form of Christianity that wanted to force everyone into a mold. Accountability was for weak people who couldn't make intelligent decisions on their own. Of course, he did feel that when issues with the artist and his band needed to be worked out, they'd come together and resolve them. But there was no need for such a legalistic view of Christian living as "accountability."

His response sounded pretty good at the time. But it collapsed like a house of cards when Bill learned six months later that the musician's wife was divorcing him, his band was leaving him, and his career was pretty much over—because for months and even years he'd been sleeping around with women he met in his travels.

What, then, is accountability? I believe accountability is *the willing decision to abide by certain agreed-upon standards, and the voluntary submission of oneself to a review by others in which one's performance is evaluated in light of those standards.*

Notice four important aspects to this definition. First, accountability is *voluntary.* Only cults demand a loyalty in which there is not willing commitment. By contrast, true accountability is a voluntary submission to others in whom you place trust.

Consequently, accountability involves a *decision* on your part, a choice as to the nature and extent of your involvement in the relationship. It's also a choice to submit to a review by others.

A third important distinctive is that accountability assumes there will be some *standards for performance.* There's a certain level of expectations involved, without which commitment becomes meaningless.

Finally, accountability involves a *review* of performance. Somewhere along the line, one must account for one's actions and allow others to determine whether one has met the standards.

Do you want to follow through with the goals you designed in Chapter 11? Then I encourage you to make yourself liable for that follow-through to at least one other person, preferably several others. For instance, hand them a written copy of your five goals; set a time to get back together and see how you're doing. It'll be hard to "blow off" your commitments if you know someone's going to be checking on you.

DECISIONS AND PROBLEMS

In addition to accountability, attaching yourself to a group as a part of your growth offers you a valuable resource for making wise decisions and solving problems creatively and courageously.

I know a man who was approached by his supervisor about the possibility of applying for a position in another department. She told him that it would mean more pay and better career opportunities. So he made inquiries, only to learn that the deadline for applying had just passed.

He would have let it go at that, but his supervisor kept after him about it, finally telling him, "Look, just go ahead and fill out the application and postdate it. I know that you're a cinch to get the job!" The man said he didn't feel right about doing that, so the supervisor said, with some frustration, "Then just fill out the form and leave the date off and give it to me. I'll take care of it from there!"

So that's what he did. Within a matter of weeks, he was awarded the new job. He'd forgotten about the incident until he got involved in a group discussion on the topic of integrity, which I attended. During the discussion, his conscience began to bother him, so he told his story to the group, wondering what he should do now that he was well-established in the position.

As you can well imagine, the group had plenty of constructive input to give him! They all understood his situation, and they had insights and creative ideas about ways he could deal with the circumstances with some integrity. He still had to make choices and take action. But the group proved invaluable in that decision-making process.

ENCOURAGEMENT

One of the values of a group is its ability to affirm and encourage. That's what the wrestling team did for me, both in practices and at matches—they cheered me on to victory. What a powerful motivation words and gestures of encouragement can be—especially when you feel discouraged and ready to throw in the towel.

I know of a group in North Dallas that has been like a shelter in a hurricane for a group of men in real estate. Recently the Texas economy has had its back broken by a plunge in oil prices and the subsequent loss of investment funds. Bank closures are at an all-time high. And the real estate industry has been in a depression, with massive layoffs, foreclosures, and bankruptcies.

The men in the group have been at the vortex of this storm. They all know friends whose fortunes have been fractioned and whose lives have been shattered by the downturn. And most of these men have also experienced severe financial losses. Yet so far they've held together, personally and spiritually. Why?

I think if you asked them, they'd tell you that their group, which meets every Friday morning, is a main stabilizing factor. These men share their victories and failures, joys and pain, hopes and fears. They counsel together, laugh together, cry together, and most importantly, pray together. They've built a bond of loyalty, affirmation, and encouragement that seems to be far stronger than the worst misfortunes of the economy.

HOW CAN YOU FORM SUCH A GROUP?

A group that includes accountability, resources for decision making, and encouragement may or may not appeal to you. For some people, a group just doesn't seem to work, or else it doesn't fit with their style or schedules. But if you want to form such a group, how do you get started? Here are a few suggestions.

Recruit a homogeneous group of peers.
Try to find people who share your values and know your world. Most likely, such persons will be in your same occupation or profession. If you're a truck driver, look for other truck drivers who want to grow in their faith. If you're a secretary, look for other secretaries. If you're a doctor, find other doctors. If you're an executive, seek out other executives.

The point here is not to be exclusive or prejudiced. It's just that growth groups tend to work better when the participants have much in common. A single parent in a clerical position who is trying to understand what it means to put her faith to work in those circumstances will do much better in a group of other single parents than with a group of senior-level managers for a Fortune 500 company.

Of course, the main thing each of the group participants needs to have in common is a serious commitment to grow in Christian faith.

Agree on the purpose and expectations of the group.
One of the main reasons groups fall apart is if there is confusion over expectations. If one person has merely a passing interest in involvement, while another person shares much of her life around the group, the two will frustrate each other.

That's why it's important, up front, before any commitments are made or expected, for the group to decide together issues such as: Why are we getting together as a group? What do we hope to accomplish? Why do we need this group? Why this group, and not some other means of growth? What will the format of the group be? What issues will we discuss? Is someone designated as a leader? If so, what are his or her responsibilities? Is there any outside work or preparation involved? How large will the group be allowed to grow? What criteria will be used to choose prospective participants? What's the time commitment? When and where will we meet? Is there a termination point for the group?

The point in working these things out is to adjust everyone's expectations prior to getting the group started. People need to know what they're committing themselves to. They have to know, if they are to follow through on their commitment.

By the way, I suggest you ask people to commit to only six or eight weeks at a time. This gives them the option of leaving the group if necessary. And most people are more likely to make limited commitments rather than open-ended ones.

Use a tool designed to accomplish the purpose of the group.

I'm assuming that the main purpose of your group will be Christian growth in each of the five areas of the Pentathlon. To that end, Bill and I have included a discussion guide in the back of this book that your group can use to help you apply the Pentathlon.

But whether you use our discussion guide or some other resource, select a tool that will accomplish your group's purpose. I don't recommend getting a group together with no structure, and no agenda, and no direction. A gathering like that can have value, but not on a long-term basis. Without a tool like a book or a discussion guide, conversation will tend to ramble superficially and cover only the pet topics of the stronger participants.

Emphasize the application of the Bible to life.
A small group is an ideal forum to accomplish such application. As the participants interact, each person will bring insight and creative suggestions for practicing biblical principles. In your group, you not only want to learn more about the Bible; you want help in putting more of the Bible to work in your own life. So keep the emphasis on the practical. The question you always want to answer is, "Okay, so what difference does all this make?"

GETTING STARTED

Are you ready to get a group going? We've mentioned a few advantages and suggestions for getting the group up and running. Now it's up to you to pull the group together. List below the names of people you think might be interested in such a group:

_____   _____

_____   _____

_____   _____

_____   _____

_____   _____

Is one of the people on the list an especially good prospect? Maybe he's a close friend or someone you're sure will want to get a group started. Mention this idea to him first, and let him brainstorm additional names with you.

Next, determine a time when you're going to contact each person on the list about forming such a group. You may be able to handle this over the phone, but most likely you'll need to explain it in person. That will mean arranging a time to meet with each person on the list. When will those times be? Write them in your date book or somewhere to remind you to meet with them. This process of getting together with prospective group members will probably take several weeks, especially if you have eight or ten names on the list or if you don't see these people every day.

When you present the idea, explain why you think a group would be helpful and who else you're considering for involvement. Solicit the names of prospects from each person and see if you can get the others to help recruit. You should also show prospects any materials that you're planning to use, such as this book. Let them know when and where an initial informational meeting will be held. Be sure to remind them of that meeting again before it takes place.

At the first meeting make sure everyone gets acquainted with one another. Then explain why you feel a group would be helpful, relating your own motivations and concerns for forming such a group. Ask others about their needs for support. This should lead into a discussion of many of the questions listed earlier about the purpose of the group and the expectations involved.

As a group, try to come to a consensus about the nature of the group and level of involvement demanded, as well as agreement on any materials that will be used. Then determine a time and place to meet that will work for everyone, and conclude the meeting (on time!).

By the way, out of eight or ten people who show an initial interest, you may end up with only four or five who want to go ahead with the group. That's okay. The size of the group is not what will make it or break it, but rather the consensus of purpose and the common commitment to make the experience work by those who do get involved.

CHAPTER THIRTEEN

Y: Use Yardsticks to Measure Your Progress

Anyone with children knows how fun it is to put a growth chart on a wall or door somewhere and periodically mark off how many inches they've grown over several months. Over the years, it's exciting to see them spurt up on the chart as they lengthen into full-bodied teens. And it's encouraging to them as they observe their physical progress; it can give them a tremendous feeling of accomplishment.

We need similar yardsticks to mark personal progress. Such records can be very encouraging as we look back over ground we've covered and victories we've won. Let me describe three strategies you can use as *yardsticks* to measure your progress.

CHARTS AND CHECKLISTS

One tool for tracking your goals is a checklist. Say, for instance, that at the beginning of each week you write down five goals that you'd like to accomplish during the week, one for each category of the Pentathlon:

•I'm going to memorize Psalm 139 as a way to remind myself of God's unique and special concern for me.

•I'm going to give my wife Thursday night off by cooking dinner and sitting with the kids. She'll be free to do whatever she'd like to do.

•I'm going to have lunch on Wednesday with Jim, a vendor for our company, and ask him if he'd like to know how to have a personal relationship with Christ.

•I'm going to call Ted, an elder in our church, and ask him what specific ways I can pray for the church.

•I'm going to buy a book called *Beyond Hunger* in order to start acquainting myself with the problem of hunger and starvation.

Five goals, neatly listed, perhaps on a three-by-five card that you'll keep on your desk or in your appointment book. As you go through the week, this checklist will serve as a reminder. And as you accomplish these goals, you'll have the satisfaction of checking them off. By the end of the week you'll be able to measure your accomplishments and get started on new goals for the next week.

Imagine using a checklist like this over a period of time. You'd never worry about whether you're getting anywhere in your faith. Instead, you'd be able to look back through your cards and point out specific, tangible steps you've taken toward Christlikeness. Your faith would become very practical. It would also start making a noticeable, measurable difference in your life.

A variation of this checklist is a chart, something like the one that follows:

DAILY CHECKLIST, Week of _____

GOALS	SUNDAY	MONDAY	TUESDAY	WEDNESDAY	THURSDAY	FRIDAY	SATURDAY	OKAY
PERSONAL LIFE 1. Memorize Psalm 139.	Memorize verses 1-6	Review	Memorize verses 7-12	Review	Memorize verses 13-18	Review	Memorize verses 19-24	
2. Work out three times this week.		Work out		Work out			Work out	
FAMILY 1. Give my wife Thursday night off.	Schedule Thursday				Give wife night off			
2. Basketball with Kirk.	Schedule w/Kirk						Basketball w/Kirk, 10:00	
WORK 1. Lunch with Jim on Wednesday.		Call Jim to schedule		Lunch with Jim, 11:45				
2. Attend training seminar.		Check schedule			Attend seminar			
CHURCH 1. Call Ted about prayer needs.			Call Ted					
2. Talk with kids' Sunday school teachers.	Visit SS after church							
COMMUNITY 1. Buy *Beyond Hunger.*							Go to bookstore	
2. Have Smiths over for snacks.	Invite Smiths for snacks							

A JOURNAL

For some people, charts and checklists are ideal. For others, they seem too mechanical. If that's the case for you, you may feel comfortable with a more reflective approach. In that case, I'd suggest keeping a journal of some sort.

A journal can be elaborate or simple, extensive or abbreviated. You can get a fancy three-ring leather binder with neatly typed index pages, or use a ninety-five-cent spiral notebook. You can even keep it on your personal computer, if you're so inclined.

Whatever format you choose, what you're after in keeping a journal is a written record of your thoughts, your questions, your conclusions, your prayers, and your intentions in regard to your Christian growth. You might want to organize such a journal around the five categories of the Pentathlon. Or you may want to use the A-P-P-L-Y acronym to divide the sections.

If you've never kept a journal, my suggestion is that each day you start a new page by answering three fundamental questions: (1) What progress did I make yesterday toward Christlikeness in my personal and spiritual life, my home, my work, my church, and my community? (2) What can I do today to become more like Christ? (3) What am I learning about God—His nature and character, His will, and my relationship to Him?

In time you'll be able to look back and trace the highs and lows of your journey. You'll also have some valuable data for troubleshooting problems that occur, as well as a history of what you've done right. Most importantly, you'll have a regular, natural, personalized means of evaluating yourself before the Lord, and of bringing problems, needs, and requests before Him.

RETREATS

One of the best ways I know of to measure your progress is periodically to get away from your routine for a time of reflection, evaluation, planning, and prayer—especially prayer.

You may not have a cabin or lake house to go to for this—but you may be able to borrow or rent one, or perhaps drive to a small town nearby where you can get a hotel room or bed-and-breakfast lodgings. The point is, find a way to break your routine and get away from your normal surroundings. Doing so will get your mind out of its customary paths of thought and provide an opportunity to gain perspective.

By the way, if you are married, you might want to include your spouse, just the two of you, and work through the following exercises, both separately and together.

Structure your retreat in order to give appropriate time to these three critical areas.

Evaluate the recent past.
Reflect back over the past six months to a year. What have been the high points? The lows? What lessons have you learned? List four or five major things about which you can feel encouraged. Then list four or five things on which you need to work.

Evaluate your current status.
This would be a good time to go through the personal inventory in Chapter 10 again, or something like it. Analyze your attitudes and behaviors in each of the five categories of the Pentathlon. As you reflect on each area, ask, "What is God telling me to do in this area? Where do I need to make changes?"

As you begin to uncover areas for growth, determine some overall objectives on which you'd like to concentrate in the next six months to a year. For instance,

"I want to pursue a real sense of intimacy with my wife this year," or "I need to get a better handle on my ethics at work this year," or "I want to grow more compassionate toward the needs of the poor this year."

Then use the goal-setting process in Chapter 11 to break these objectives down into specific action steps that you'll carry out when you return home.

Pray.
Leave plenty of time for prayer. You might want to preface this time by reading a portion of Scripture that describes God's character. Then begin by praising God for His attributes and for what He has done. Thank Him for the specific ways in which He has helped you and your family during the previous year.

Then confess ways in which you have failed Him. Be as specific as possible. Thank Him for His compassion, His grace, and His forgiveness.

Finally, pray about the discoveries of your retreat. Thank God for the victories, and ask for His help in overcoming weaknesses. Pray about your objectives and goals in each of the five areas, asking for wisdom, strength, and the disciplines and courage to follow through. Pray about anything else that you feel is important.

If you take such a retreat and seriously work through these exercises, I can almost guarantee you'll return to your world with a sense of renewal, a sense of hope, and a confidence that God is with you. You'll gain a sense of perspective, both in your work and in non-work areas. Most importantly, you'll have a renewed walk with God, having worshiped Him and brought your life before Him.

CHAPTER FOURTEEN

Watch Out for the Enemy!

While I never served in combat duty in the Vietnam War, I was sent to Southern Asia for a brief period as an intelligence officer. My job was to brief Air Force pilots in the suspected or known placement of enemy anti-aircraft artillery ("Triple-A").

As you can well imagine, every pilot at the intelligence briefings strained to hear me map out coordinates of the enemy and other data on which their very lives depended. The only exception was one old boy who was just too cool to pay attention to a smooth-cheeked lieutenant like me.

I specifically remember that I called out the placement of some "Triple-A" one day and noticed that this cowboy was catnapping in the back row. Sure enough, later that day, he flew right over that enemy position and was shot down. It took the rest of that day for our gunships and several squads of rescuers to pull him out of the jungle and return him safely back to our base.

I watched him as he swaggered in, accepting handshakes and slaps on the back from all of his companions, as if he'd done something brave. He was in his glory, but I thought, "You fool! You didn't pay attention to that briefing this morning. As a result you lost an expensive plane, risked the lives of dozens of men who had to rescue you, and could have died!"

As we draw this discussion of balancing competing time demands to a conclusion, I need to give you some "intelligence" about two very potent dangers that can bring you down. And I hope you won't be like that foolish pilot, who nearly came to ruin by ignoring some simple advice.

As you attempt to bring your life into biblical balance, you'll want to avoid two common fallacies: beware of trying to become like Christ through merely human effort; and beware of legalism. These problems are related. And both will destroy your spiritual life. Let me explain.

BEWARE OF MERELY HUMAN EFFORT!

Sometimes when people hear about the A-P-P-L-Y concept of Christian growth, they get the idea that becoming Christlike happens through merely human effort. That's a misperception.

Even our best efforts to live the way God wants us to will fall pitifully short of Christ's matchless perfection. A husband could serve his wife with genuine humility and sacrifice; yet how could he ever love her to the same degree "as Christ loved the church" (Ephesians 5:25)? A worker could do his work with all the excellence he can muster and even endure the injustices of a vicious employer; yet would he ever fully match the perfect example of Christ and completely "follow in His steps" (1 Peter 2:21)?

In that case, you might ask, what's the point of trying? Alexander Graham Bell, the inventor, had a seminal and lasting influence on the founding and direction of the National Geographic Society and its outstanding publication, *National Geographic*. Bell fathered two daughters, but no sons. One of his daughters, Elsie May, married Gilbert H. Grosvenor, the first editor of the magazine and director of the society. In 1901 Gilbert and Elsie gave Bell his first grandson, whom they named Melville, and the boy became the son that Bell never had.

The two spent hours together in Bell's study, the inventor masterminding various projects, the boy studying his school lessons. Occasionally they worked on something together. One such joint venture was the construction of a toy steamboat made from an egg, powered by a candle.

Now picture these two people working together on this project. One is a world-class inventor whose work includes breakthroughs related to the telephone, the telegraph, the phonograph, the "photophone," a metal detection probe, the iron lung, the tetrahedron, the airplane, hydrofoil boats, the audiometer, and a host of other devices, to say nothing of his contributions in fields as diverse as phonics and genetics. The other is a boy enjoying an intriguing new venture. Which of their efforts accounts for that toy boat?

The answer is *both* were intensively involved! Melville was no doubt captivated by the new invention, by the creative process and the careful construction of the boat. However, fueling this passionate interest was the pleasure he must have felt at seeing the old man's smile, feeling his affection and affirmation, and sensing his interest. But Bell was no less enthusiastic about the project. His love of inventions, no matter how small or seemingly insignificant, certainly captivated him. But far more engaging was his deep love and intimacy with his grandson. He must have delighted to see the boy's delight, and though this project was a trifle compared with his other work, the relationship itself caused him to invest as much interest and energy in it as if it were as important as the telephone.

This is analogous to our walk with Christ and to our growth toward Christlikeness. All of our specific, measurable, achievable, and compatible action steps are in some ways like little toy steamboats—mere trifles when compared to the perfect work of Christ. Yet because of our relationship to Him—because He loves us deeply and delights to see us grow—He invests our efforts with meaning and power. In fact, if we'll let Him, He becomes the Mastermind behind our life and the power working in and with and through our own feeble efforts to make us like Himself.

So we never want to think that Christian growth means humans accomplishing amazing things on God's behalf. Rather, it's a process of Christ, through His Holy Spirit, accomplishing amazing things in and through us, both for His sake and ours. Confusion on this point can lead to no end of trouble and frustration.

BEWARE OF LEGALISM!

A related danger is *legalism*, thinking that Christian growth is merely a matter of doing the right things. Certainly we should do the right things, but it's important to understand why and in what way.

In an earlier chapter I responded to the question, "If the A-P-P-L-Y strategy for Christian growth is biblical, why is there no specific Bible verse that presents that strategy?" I argued that there is no one authoritative way to grow in the faith outlined anywhere in Scripture. Life is too complicated for that, and people are too diverse. Instead, I offered the A-P-P-L-Y concept as my best effort at summarizing some biblical principles of growth that have been helpful for many.

But there's another reason, I think, why God doesn't prescribe any particular method. Let's suppose that I could show you a passage that named five steps of Christian growth—all laid out in a nice acronym, *A-P-P-L-Y*. How would you respond? I think most people would think, "This is wonderful! If I just do these five steps, then I'll please God."

What's wrong with that? Well, imbedded in that thinking is a subtle error that has plagued followers of God since the beginning, the error of *legalism*. Legalism is the idea that "God accepts me because of what I've done." Of course, the converse of this is also legalism: "God does not accept me because of what I've done (or failed to do)."

Either way, if you think like this, it sets you on an attempt to prove to God that you are worthy of His acceptance and deserving of His love. You'll relate to God on the basis of your moral performance, trying to earn His favor.

In short, you'll set up a deal with God, by which He'll owe you His love in return for your good behavior. Conversely, if you fail before Him, you'll deserve His judgment and punishment.

This way of thinking is called legalism because it's a relationship with God based on law, not on grace. The "law" here is some image you have of a moral law against which God is measuring you. That moral law may be expressed for you through the Ten Commandments, the

Golden Rule, the Sermon on the Mount, or even the harsh, unrealistic standards of a neurotic parent.

Whatever the source, if you're a legalist, you'll try to live up to ever higher, impossibly demanding expectations. You'll constantly be comparing yourself to others, condemning yourself when you fall short of someone else's achievements, and condemning others when they violate your standards. You'll also live with guilt, constantly weighed down by a sense of God's displeasure and disapproval. And quite likely you'll nurse a subterranean rage at God that despite your best efforts, He has somehow not lived up to His end of the bargain.

What a wretched way to live! That could start to happen to you if you misunderstand the A-P-P-L-Y concept. You'll need to keep the following points in mind:

1. God never accepts you because of what you do, but because of what He has done for you in Christ. God owes you *nothing*! He never has and never will, no matter what you do or don't do.

2. The basis of our relationship with God is His grace. This is really the heart of the matter, which legalists misunderstand. They think they're relating to God on the basis of performance. But Scripture clearly teaches that when there was nothing we could do to regain a relationship with God, God did everything necessary to reestablish that possibility. That's grace. (See Romans 5:6-11, Ephesians 2:1-10.) All we need to do is respond to His grace.

3. As for obedience to God, that is vitally important—not as a basis for our relationship with God, but rather as a loving expression of that relationship.

Legalists confuse the means with the ends. They believe that adherence to standards somehow wins God's favor. They think that right conduct is what ultimately matters. Right conduct becomes an end in itself.

But the end that we should pursue is to know and love God. Right conduct may and will result from that, but it's an expression of our gratitude, not an attempt to win God's favor. We should seek to please God, not in order to establish our relationship with Him, but because He has already established it in Christ.

4. Another reason for obeying Christ is that in obeying Him, we become like Him. And that's God's goal for us. He brings us into right relation with Himself in order to make us into a certain kind of people—people of high moral character, of courage, of joy, of inner freedom, of faith, of health. He wants to make us into people who, through their unique personalities, display Christ.

5. The A-P-P-L-Y strategy is merely a tool to help you become more like Christ. Many have found it to be useful. But you may not. Checklists and personality inventories and accountability groups may not fit your personality or style. That's okay. Use other approaches if they help you more. But by all means seek to know Christ and strive for a character that pleases Him!

CHAPTER FIFTEEN

This All Sounds Good, But . . .

Are you a professing believer but a practicing skeptic? Do you affirm the great doctrines of the Christian faith, only to doubt whether they really can make much difference in your day-to-day life? Do you applaud those who articulate God's truth with style and flair, only to plead mitigating circumstances when it comes to applying that truth yourself?

Unfortunately, this is the case for too many people. Too many of us are practicing skeptics. We say we believe God and want to obey Him; but then we turn around and offer excuses: "Oh, but you don't know my circumstances"; "I'm sure this works for most people, but I'm different"; "My life's just not that simple"; or "I've never been able to make it work for me." In short, we deflect the impact of biblical teaching by somehow completing a sentence that begins, "This all sounds good, but . . . ."

When it comes to balancing competing time demands. I've found that some people seem to offer their demographic profile as a reason why the Pentathlon and the A-P-P-L-Y strategy can't help them. It's as if they think God's truth can't keep up with modern life! Let me address myself, then, to the particulars of several categories of workers, beginning with working fathers.

I'M A BUSY FATHER

I'm a busy father. So is Bill. And so are many of the hundreds of people who have found this material to be helpful. If you're a busy husband and father, you especially need to keep work in its proper perspective, because so many lives are depending on you.

Men, I know it's a tough world out there! I know the implications of placing limits on your career demands. I know the strong attraction of career success. I know you face a tough, secular environment that is often brutally competitive and without sympathy. And I know how much success at work affects your feelings of significance and worth as a man.

I also know how difficult it is to keep all the balls in the air as you juggle work and family, church and community—to say nothing of your own sanity! So here are some suggestions especially for busy fathers:

1. Make up your mind that no matter what the cost, you're going to make Christ the Lord over every aspect of your life, beginning with your work. If that costs you a few rungs on the career ladder, so be it. Of course, it may not; it may actually help you do a better job at work. But either way, determine that Christ is going to be your Lord and not just the caboose on a train driven by career success.

2. If possible, set a regular time when you'll leave work and go home.

3. As you pull in your driveway and walk to the front door, remind yourself that you're coming home to serve,

not to be served. I call this time *reentry*. It's a delicate period late in the day, when you're tired, your wife is tired, and if you have young children, they're probably going bonkers! I suggest that when you arrive home, you observe the "stand-up rule." The stand-up rule says that in that late afternoon or early evening, between, say, 5:00-7:30, whenever you see your wife standing up—for whatever reason—you'll stand up as well. This may sound corny, but try it. You may be amazed at the difference it makes, both in your attitude (as a servant) and your wife's (as the one being served).

4. Review the five areas of the Pentathlon weekly with your spouse. Plan your weekly schedule together and help each other devise goals. Then keep track of your progress together during the week.

5. Avoid pursuing a lifestyle of luxury, and if possible, stay out of debt. Nothing will keep you (and your spouse) chained to your work like extravagance and credit purchases. If you're pursuing a lifestyle of comfort and convenience, you're pursuing a very secular lifestyle.

6. I strongly encourage you to form a small group of peers as described in Chapter 12. Men are notorious "lone rangers" when it comes to growing in Christ. But they need the friendship and accountability of other men. Don't try to go it alone. Surround yourself with other men who can get to know you well and be a resource in the struggles of being busy men.

7. Work especially hard at learning to communicate your emotions to your spouse and to other men. If this is a problem for you, don't be ashamed to get some professional counsel to help you deal with your feelings.

8. Take pains to assist your wife and children in household chores. Many men who are the major bread-

winners in their families take the view, "I'm paying for all of this, so let my wife and kids keep the house!" That's not a servant attitude. Don't be too proud or busy to accept a significant portion of the domestic responsiblities. Perhaps it would help for you and your family to make a list of everything that needs to be done, and then divide up the tasks so everyone can finish them sooner and get on with the fun side of life.

9. If your wife works outside the home, be sure to read through the two sections that follow. If she is at home full-time, be sure to read through the section on career homemakers.

I'M A WORKING MOTHER

The phenomenon of large numbers of women in the workplace is barely twenty years old. And, frankly, it's taken the Church by surprise. Christian teachers haven't yet come to a consensus, either theologically or practically, in addressing the many issues of women in the workplace. About the only message given with any strong voice is, "Mothers shouldn't be working!" If you're a mother who must work, that's not very helpful.

I can't address all the complex issues involved in the debate about working women, but here are a few suggestions.

1. If you have preschool children, I recommend that you not work unless you absolutely have to—and I do mean *absolutely!* The first four or five years of life are incredibly formative and determinative. There's no way to rationalize around the fact that God intends children to be with their mothers during that period.

Of course, if your family's survival is at stake, you probably have no choice but to work. Nor should you feel ashamed or second class because you must work. God knows your situation, and I believe He is pleased to see your willingness to support your family and meet their needs.

Survival, however, is one thing; working only to pay for a lifestyle of comfort and convenience is something else—something I believe is detestable in God's sight. If you are sacrificing your children and your relationship to them on the altar of extravagant mortgage payments or exotic vacations, then your values are twisted. There is a great difference between survival needs and luxury. As a mother, you'll want to think long and hard about what your family really needs, both materially and relationally, and where your responsibilities lie in both of those areas.

Don't let pressures about fulfilling yourself through a career distract you from fulfilling your obligations as a mother. I'm not saying women shouldn't work or seek the satisfactions that employment can provide, but keep in mind that life is given to us for far more than our own fulfillment. We all need to learn the Christlike fulfillment that comes from serving others, including our children.

2. If you work, acknowledge the fact that fatigue and time pressure will be your two biggest problems. For this reason, you'll need to arrange with your husband (attention, men!) a regular period when you can take time out and just do something you want to do, by yourself. This might be an evening or a weekend afternoon, while your husband cares for the children.

3. Because of the pressure you're under, it's especially important that you take steps to keep a fresh, vibrant walk with God. You need to experience His presence *daily*. Otherwise, it's inevitable that you'll feel

bitterness and anger and lose perspective.

4. Recognize that your work may take its toll, to some degree, on your relationships at home. This is not insurmountable, but it's an ever-present danger you'll want to guard against.

5. Avoid going into debt in order to work, or because you work. I've known women who justify buying a whole new wardrobe or a new car just because they've landed a job—even if the wardrobe or car is not necessary—and they go into debt to pay for them. Sometimes they think, "Well, now that I've got a job, I can spend some money on myself," and rack up credit purchases right and left. Either way, this is not a biblical view of work or lifestyle.

6. Of all the kinds of tasks a working mother might do, the one I'd recommend least is starting a business. Typically that will require sixty-five to seventy or more hours a week. The only way to find that amount of time is to rob your children of their mother's presence.

7. By all means make sure that your children are never without responsible adult supervision—*especially* if they are teenagers. That doesn't mean that someone must always be with them or looking over their shoulders. But you don't want your children wandering around the streets, the malls, their friends' bedrooms— without someone's knowledge and oversight.

8. Because both you and your husband work, a practical matter you may need to decide together is which of your careers will take priority.

9. Like any worker, you'll need to set a time to return home from work.

10. Like your husband, you'll need to prepare mentally for reentry when you arrive home. Remember, though you're tired and ready to call it quits, you're there

as a servant, not as someone to be served. This has nothing to do with your being a woman; it has everything to do with your being a follower of Christ.

WE'RE A TWO-CAREER COUPLE

In addition to all the suggestions listed in the two categories above, two-career couples, with or without children, will need to consider a number of additional factors.

1. The greatest enemy of your marriage is the tendency for work interests, career responsibilities, and job relationships to pull you apart. You can both become so wrapped up in your careers that you have neither time nor energy—and eventually no interest—left for each other.

Genesis 1:26-27 paints a picture of marriage as a partnership. Given the strong emphasis in that same passage on humans as workers with God, it is clear that marriage is to be a partnership in all dimensions of life, including work.

This implies that the work husbands and wives do, whether it's work inside or outside the home, is to be done in partnership. Not that you do the same job or work for the same company, but you should both share as much as you can in each other's work life. You should become knowledgeable about your spouse's work and how he or she feels about it. You should be supportive and helpful to your spouse as a worker. You may also become involved socially with those with whom your spouse works.

2. At the same time, you'll want to guard against letting all your conversation be dominated by work and work-related topics. Remember, life is more than work.

3. Two-career couples often display a subtle tendency toward selfishness. Perhaps it's their preoccupation with their careers. Perhaps it's the affluence their double incomes often supply. At any rate, you'll want to avoid letting your lives revolve around your jobs to the exclusion of service to others.

This is a distinct temptation for couples without children. When they come home at the end of a tough day, they may want to shut out the world and relax and pursue their own interests. In fact, they may see this as their reward for having worked so hard.

However, this conflicts with our purpose as Christ's followers to be servants of people. If you don't have children, then your time off from work should not be put only into serving yourself, but into serving others, perhaps through your church or in the community. Obviously, you have personal needs that need to be cared for. But you'll want to put at least as much energy into meeting the needs of others as you put into meeting your own.

If you have children, you'll need to avoid the strong tendency to force them to take a back seat to your work. Not that your children run the show and never make sacrifices, but the one sacrifice they should never have to make is a relationship with their parents that ultimately is more valuable than any job or career success.

I'M A CAREER HOMEMAKER

If you're a woman at home full-time—what I call a career homemaker—you have one of the most demanding jobs there is. In fact, because your work and home and family are virtually indistinguishable, you are especially vulnerable to letting your job consume your entire life. For that reason, you must pay special attention to keeping things in their proper perspective.

Let me affirm the dignity of what you do—particularly if you care for children. You have been given the incredible privilege of being Jesus to the youngsters God has given you. Your hands are the hands of Christ for them. Your smile is His smile, your eyes His eyes, your voice His voice. You occupy a position in the lives of your children that no one else ever can or will. So never think that you're "just" a mother. As a mother, you have a unique opportunity to pour the love and nurture and discipline of the Lord directly into the lives of some important people at a formative point in their growth.

Here are a few suggestions for managing it all.

1. Beware of allowing your emotional commitment to your family to rule your life. Since I'm neither a woman nor a mother, I may be suggesting the impossible here. But it's my observation that many mothers expend all of their emotional energy in caring for their families. I question whether that is healthy.

I know how easy it is for people who work outside the home to become driven by their work, consumed by it because it dominates their emotional life. And we rightly point out the unhealthiness of that. But if that can happen outside the home, I believe it can happen even more to someone whose work *is* the home and family. After all, what could be more emotionally gripping than our marriages and our children?

Furthermore, there is a strong emphasis in Christian circles today on the family. This is a good thing, on the whole. But just as we can get work out of perspective with the rest of life, so we can get our family out of perspective with where it fits into the rest of life. And this is a special danger for career homemakers. So I urge you to guard your use of emotional energy.

One way that this shows up is if your relationship to your husband routinely gets supplanted by your relationship to your children. I'm aware of men who rarely enjoy an intelligent conversation with their wives, rarely spend time alone with them, and rarely have sex with them—not because the husbands don't want to and not because the wives are incapable of these functions, but because the women give all of their time, all of their physical strength, and all of their emotional energy to their children. There's just nothing left over for their husbands.

A similar symptom is if a mother is too busy taking care of her husband, her children, the chores, and so on to spend time daily with the Lord. We all recognize that a mother has precious few moments to devote to prayer and quiet time with God. But if it's a case of the "too busies"—if you're too busy to worship God each day—you're too busy.

2. That brings us to a second suggestion: Guard time for yourself and for your relationship with God. As for the latter, your role and responsibilities in the home are far too important for you to neglect a close, intimate communion with God every day.

"But how can I possibly find the time?" you may be wondering. I suppose that depends on you and your specific situation. One woman may be able to rise in the morning a half hour before her family—fifteen minutes to wake up with a cup of coffee, and another fifteen minutes reading a psalm and praying. Another woman may choose to schedule this time at the end of her day, once things are quiet. Others may grab a moment or two while a child naps, or perhaps for twenty minutes just after her children have left for school, or while she's waiting to pick them up in the afternoon.

When Bill was a child, his mother routinely spent a few minutes in prayer each morning before the family woke up. Later, as she went about her chores, she left her Bible open on the kitchen counter, and whenever she would pass by, she'd review a verse for a moment. Then, while she folded laundry or ironed or drove to the grocery store, she would mull over the verse and its implications in her mind. Needless to say, she got a lot of Bible study in that way and, better yet, thought up countless ways to apply the truths to her life.

There's no question that time is a mother's most precious possession. But there can also be no question that a mother needs time each day with her Lord. Whatever it takes to carve out that time, do it!

But also arrange for time just for yourself. You may need to work this out with your husband, as far as supervising the children. But a mother, like any other worker, needs respite from her work, which in her case means time away from her husband and kids. I suppose the ideal would be a daily "time out" period. But life being what it is today, that break may come only once a week.

However often it occurs, career homemakers need to avoid letting their work/home responsibilities keep them from attending to their personal life and interests.

3. In a career homemaker's job, relationships will almost always need to take precedence over tasks. This is unlike most job situations, which are inherently task-oriented. But a home is relationally-oriented. It's a place for expressing and exploring feelings, a place for experimenting with and trying new things, a place for learning, and consequently a place where failure must be allowed. A mother's job is largely to oversee and nurture

this relational dynamic.

Consequently, I recommend that if you're a mother, you emphasize relationships over tasks. In practical terms, this means it's far more important that you work at building healthy children than that you keep a spotless home. There is nothing wrong with a clean home. But what good is a spotless floor if the children who walk on it don't know who they are, don't feel accepted, and don't know how to relate to others.

4. This leads to a fourth suggestion: Learn as much as you can about biblical parenting. This is especially important if your own parents were inadequate role models. There is a host of outstanding materials available from experts like Jim Dobson and his organization, Focus on the Family. Your local Christian bookstore will have many resources available, and your pastor can doubtless tell you where to find more.

The point is to become something of an expert yourself in the growth and development of your children, and the part you and your husband play in that process. Your job is in part to raise godly, healthy children, so do everything you can to learn to do that job with excellence.

5. As for your husband, make sure you leave time to spend with him. He needs that time—and so do you. If at all possible, you should arrange for baby-sitting once a week in order to date your husband. Learn about his work—not only what he does and why, but what his feelings are about his job, what issues he deals with day-to-day, and who some of the important people are.

6. You probably need to be the keeper of the family schedule. As such, you'll often play the role of a traffic cop, coordinating who goes where, when, and by what means. This requires that you'll need to keep up with

your husband's schedule, as well as think through how your children's activities affect family life—to say nothing of your own plans.

7. Finally, if it's not painfully obvious by now, you'll need to work extra hard at organizing life for yourself and your family. this is a terribly important function, though it won't win any awards. But there are so many things flowing through a home—activities, chores, purchases, people to be attended to, celebrations to be planned, traditions to be maintained—that someone needs to pay attention to how it all fits together. That's likely to be you.

Obviously many events in a family occur spontaneously. But if you want to achieve some efficiency and keep things running smoothly, you'll need to get organized. That might mean keeping a master calendar. But it can also mean lists of all kinds—lists of groceries, of birthdays and anniversaries, of chores, of phone numbers, of baby-sitters, etc.

You can organize things however you wish. But by all means, don't let your home and family degenerate into a chaos. That would hardly achieve the excellence God wants you to put into your work.

I'M A SINGLE PARENT

If you're a single parent, you've got a tough lot in life, no doubt about it. Can you balance competing time demands? I think so. Here are a few suggestions.

1. You'll need to accept limited objectives. For most single parents, life boils down to work and children. There's not a lot of time—or energy—left over for much else, least of all for personal needs. Consequently, you'll

need to be realistic about the expectations you place on yourself.

For instance: your home or apartment probably won't win any *Good Housekeeping* awards. You may have to live with unfinished chores. You won't be able to devote hours of time to people in need. You probably won't have a lot of money to share with the poor and with Christian ministries and charitable organizations. It would be amazing if you were able to spend more than fifteen or twenty minutes alone with God each day. You'll probably feel more cross with your children than you'd like to. You may have to miss some of their events, like soccer matches or school plays, because of work.

In other words, when it comes to the five areas of the Pentathlon, you'll have to accept some limitations. You'll need to do the best you can, accepting the fact that other people in other circumstances will be able to reach the ideals that you'd like to.

However, be encouraged by the fact that God knows your situation and is gracious and kind. Sincerity of effort and devotion to Him count far more than doing all the right things. All He requires of you is that you do the best job you reasonably can to serve Him faithfully with the resources and responsibilities He's given you. If that falls short of some ideal, His grace will make up the difference.

2. For that reason, though, it's imperative that you maintain a healthy, growing relationship with Him. By all means, don't let the tensions and pressures from your children and your work keep you from at least a few moments before Him each day. You need to experience His presence!

3. You also need the support and encouragement of a small group of other single parents. Look for a church

that encourages and assists such groups. You may feel, "All I've got is myself, and I guess I'm going to have to make it on my own." But the reality is you need others who understand your situation and will stand with you in the struggle.

I'M A SINGLE PERSON

If you're single, let me tell you that married couples, especially those with children, will never believe you if you tell them you struggle with balancing time demands. You'll get no sympathy from them!

And yet I have enough single friends and acquaintances to realize that there really are time tensions for the single person.

You face the strong temptation to allow work not only to dominate your life, but to become your life! Since you don't have a spouse and children pulling you in other directions, your time, your emotional energy, your relationships, your reading, your outlook on life, your reason for existence—just about everything—can revolve around your work.

Is this healthy? Is it Christlike? I don't think so. On the basis of passages like 1 Corinthians 7:32-35, I believe a more biblical perspective is to see your singleness as a God-given opportunity to serve the Lord and other people. Obviously you'll want to do much of that through your work. But I suggest that instead of letting your career eat up all of your life, you set limits on your work and devote your free time to the Lord and others.

I know that this contrasts sharply with our culture's view of single life. But the culture's view tends toward a selfish preoccupation with career success and its rewards. It also tells you in a thousand ways that after you've worked hard, you owe it to yourself to party hard—another self-oriented pursuit.

That's a tragic waste of a valuable resource in the face of overwhelming human need. Like the rest of us, you have 168 hours a week to use. Say sixty go to sleep, forty to work, and another twenty to other tasks. That leaves about forty or fifty hours a week of extra time—time that no spouse or children or the hassles they create will take from you. Biblically, how should you use that time?

I believe you should consider taking on a "second career" that further uses your abilities as a servant for Jesus Christ. That might mean volunteering for a meals-on-wheels program. Or carrying out effective strategies to lead people to Christ. Or leading a music or drama group at your church. Or putting your vocational skills at the service of an organization assisting the poor. Or volunteering to watch a single parent's child so that she can get some much needed and appreciated free time.

In short, your time is a tremendous asset given you by God. Don't use it for merely self-centered purposes. Give it away for the sake of His Kingdom!

I'M A RETIREE

In many ways, you're in the same boat as the single person, only your boat is twice as large: instead of forty or fifty extra hours to fill up, you've got eighty or ninety.

I view the popular American concept of retirement with deep suspicion. First of all, I don't find it taught in Scripture that people should work their whole lives to build up an income and then drop out of work one day and live off their nest egg. No, I believe that God wants us to be active for Him throughout our lives. That will take different forms at different ages, but Christians should never "retire." They may conclude employment, but that should only free them for useful service elsewhere.

As with the single person, that service may take the form of volunteer work. Or it may mean putting your occupational skills to work for a ministry or relief organization. It certainly should involve giving yourself to your grandchildren, if you have any.

Whatever the form of your service, avoid the trap of using retirement only to fulfill self-centered dreams and promises. I'm not suggesting that you never play golf, or take a cruise, or buy a Winnebago and tour the country. Those kinds of activities may be exactly what you need.

But by all means, as you write the final chapters of your life, center them around a devotion to Christ and a compassionate service to people. Any other ending would be a meaningless failure, a useless waste of a precious commodity—your time.

CHAPTER SIXTEEN

Don't Stop Here!

A s an author, I hate to say it, but reading a book will not change your life. At least not much. I have a whole library at CIM headquarters packed with books. Bill has an equally impressive collection at his house. But between the two of us, I doubt that we could come up with enough titles to fill a single shelf of books that have made a substantive, noticeable, permanent difference in the way we live our lives.

Perhaps I'm overstating the case or overestimating what a book should do. But I feel compelled to warn you that *if you stop here, this book will make very little difference in your life!* I feel quite certain of that.

When it comes to balancing competing time demands, we don't just need more *ideas* on how to do that; we need a practical manual to help us *do* that. Bill and I have done our best to write this book as a manual, but if you're like most people, you'll mostly get motivated by it. Whether that translates into life change is still up in the air.

Obviously a lot depends on you. Even the most

stirring challenges and the best-designed manuals in the world can't overcome apathy or laziness. But I'm assuming you haven't read this far out of indifference. Instead, I suspect that you really do want to face this issue of time demands squarely and gain some godly control over your life.

In that case, don't stop now! If you've read this far and you're saying, "Doug, this sounds great! I want to put my work in proper perspective. So where do I get started? What's the next step?"—then keep going into the study guide that follows called "Applying the Pentathlon: A Manual for Growth."

What you'll find there is a series of questions and exercises to help you do what it takes to get started. You can work through it on your own. Better yet, team up with a group of others who also want to manage their lives and work by God's objectives.

I've watched thousands of busy people just like you go through this process and seen it change their lives. It's not the material that's so great. It's the fact that they were doing something instead of thinking about doing something. If you want life change, going through the exercises that follow is the place to get started.

By the way, don't worry that I'm signing you up for a program that you'll have to stay on for the rest of your life. The material that follows is a *start* toward building lifelong habits. The habits need to last, not this book. It's like learning to read: We all started with our A-B-C's and Dick-and-Jane primers. But in time, we left those training wheels behind because we mastered the basics.

The fact is, most people find that after working through the steps covered in the following study guide for several months, they need a break. They don't forget about honoring Christ with their lives, but they need a fresh approach at doing that. Otherwise, their goals and other strategies toward growth can become mechanical.

I suggest going through the study guide for several months, and then taking two or three months off to work with a different resource. Then come back to this guide with a fresh perspective and begin setting new goals in your life. After several years of this pattern, you'll find that the principles of applying God's Word to your life will become natural and something you do routinely. That's a point of real maturity!

So don't stop now. Turn the page and get started on a path that will put God's Word to work in your life. When you're finished, use the response card in the back of this book to write and tell me about what happened. Bill and I and the entire CIM team are praying for you, that you'll take the necessary steps to honor God with your time. Let us know how our prayers have been answered in your life, so we can all praise God together.

Now get started!

APPLYING THE PENTATHLON:
A Manual for Growth

How to Get the Most from This Guide!

The material that follows is a six-part manual to help you apply the principles in this book to your life. There's no question that while we retain very little of what we read, we retain nearly all of what we do. In the sessions that follow, you'll *do* far more than you'll read!

Here's how to gain the most from this material.

USE IT WITH A GROUP

We find that small discussion groups are an ideal way to apply biblical truth to life. That's why we've designed this for discussion, not just self-study. We strongly encourage you to interact with a group of your friends using this manual. To have an effective group, you'll need to do several things:

1. Limit the group's size to six or eight people. If you have nine or more, we recommend splitting into two groups.

2. Make sure each participant has a copy of this book.

3. Be clear as to the time and place for the discussion.

4. Clarify expectations before you begin. Everyone should agree on the purpose of the group and the level of commitment to it.

5. Set a termination date for the group, or at least for using this book. Don't ask people for open-ended commitments.

6. Appoint a discussion leader. This person is not a teacher, but someone who can facilitate a healthy group interaction.

7. Keep the discussion focused. The questions and material in this guide have been designed to help you think and talk about important issues. Don't get sidetracked. Encourage everyone to participate. This is a discussion, not a lecture or a platform for one person's point of view.

8. Come prepared to discuss. The preparation involved is minimal. Each session corresponds to sections of the book, so reading the material ahead of time will help. However, someone can easily participate in the discussion even if that person hasn't read the book.

9. We haven't left much space in this guide to write many notes, so you may find it helpful to record answers to some questions in a separate notebook or journal. This will prove especially helpful for the exercises that require extended responses and reflection.

10. Some of the questions in this guide ask for painfully honest disclosure. For example, the personal inventory in Session 3 asks you to tell about areas of your life where you feel you could be stronger. To make this kind of vulnerability possible and healthy, you must agree to maintain strict confidences, to avoid judgment, and to strive for honesty even when it's uncomfortable.

SUGGESTIONS FOR GROUP LEADERS

You have an important role to play in making this experience helpful for everyone. In any group situation, someone's got to get things rolling and keep things moving. That's your job! If you do it well, the other natural dynamics of the group process will take care of everything else.

1. Come prepared. At a minimum, this involves reading the book and previewing the particular session that your group will cover. Doing so will give you confidence and a sense of where things are headed during the discussion. Moreover, your preparation sets a vital example for the other participants. It shows them how seriously you take the group, and therefore, how seriously they should take it.

2. In preparation for Session 1, you'll need to select, from among the three stories in Chapter 2, the one that seems most relevant to your group.

3. Your goal is to keep a lively discussion going. You can do that by probing people's responses, asking for clarification, and raising thought-provoking questions. Of course, others in the group should be encouraged to do the same. Whatever you do, avoid "teaching" the content of the book.

4. Don't let someone dominate the group with his or her opinions or personality. Try to get each participant—especially shy or quiet ones—to say at least one or two things at each session.

5. Keep track of the time. Before the group meets, think through how much time should be allotted to each section of the session. That way you can keep things moving. We've designed each session to have resolution and completion, so if the last few questions or exercises

are not covered, people may feel frustrated. By the way, the ideal length of time for a discussion is an hour to an hour and fifteen minutes.

6. End the discussion on time. People have other responsibilities and commitments. If the session lasts too long, they may develop a negative attitude toward the group. By contrast, cutting off a lively interaction will bring everyone back with enthusiasm. Our rule is, "Leave them longing, not loathing!"

THIS GUIDE CAN BE USED FOR SELF-STUDY

Discussion groups won't work for everyone. That's okay. You can still enjoy valuable benefits from this guide even in self-study. Just make a couple of adjustments.

1. You'll have to be much more self-disciplined, because you won't have the built-in accountability of a group. We recommend that you determine a specific time and place to study. Then put that in your appointment book so you won't crowd it out with other commitments.

2. Since you won't have a group to discuss the material with, you'll spend a great deal of effort in personal reflection and thought. Writing (or taping) will replace discussing. However, you should seek opportunities to discuss your ideas with others—coworkers, your spouse, other Christians. These people will be invaluable in helping you gain perspective and offering you objective feedback, even though they will participate on an informal basis.

Session 1

*In this session, you'll examine
your own struggles with balancing
competing time demands.*

PART ONE
SUGGESTED TIME: 25-30 MINUTES

In Chapter 2, the stories of Frank, Sharon, and Luanne are presented. Select one of these and, after reading or reviewing it, answer the questions asked below. If one of these three people bears a resemblance to you, you'll probably want to choose that person's story.

Frank (page 21)
Frank is a busy husband and father struggling to get his life organized. After reading or reviewing his story, discuss the following questions:

1. a. Compare Frank's situation to what you think is fairly normal.

   b. Do you know anyone like Frank? If so, describe him or her.

2. Frank's whole life seems to operate in a crisis mode. Why is that?

3. How does Frank's inability to manage his life affect his relationships with . . .

his boss?

his coworkers?

his wife?

his children?

4. a. Is there hope for someone like Frank?

b. If there is, what practical changes could he make to get control of his life and schedule?

5. a. What aspects of Frank's situation can you especially relate to?

b. Why do you relate to those?

Sharon (page 24)
Sharon is a single parent struggling with responsibilities at work and at home.

1. Sharon's life is pretty much taken up by her work as a legal secretary and her responsibilities as a mother. Describe the impact of this on Sharon. How do you think it affects her . . .

physically?

emotionally?

spiritually?

2. Sharon feels that no one really understands her situation, certainly not her boss or the people at her church. Do you think most single parents are misunderstood? Why or why not?

3. What suggestions would you make to Sharon to help her balance the various demands made on her?

4. a. What aspects of Sharon's situation can you especially relate to?

   b. Why do you relate to those?

Luanne (page 28)
Luanne is a busy working mother.

1. How would you assess the impact of Luanne's job on her relationship . . .

   with her husband?

   with her children?

   with her friends?

   on herself?

2. If you know someone whose circumstances are similar to Luanne's, describe them.

3. How might Luanne avoid or reduce tensions between her job and her family?

4. How would you begin to help someone like Luanne cope with the various responsibilities she has?

5. a. What aspects of Luanne's situation can you identify with?

   b. How do you handle these things yourself?

PART TWO
SUGGESTED TIME: 20-30 MINUTES

Answer the questions on the following inventory by circling *Yes* if the statement accurately describes you or your perspective, or *No* if it does not. Don't spend too long on any one item. Usually, the first response that pops into your mind is the most accurate. When you're finished, total your answers as indicated.

1. I believe my spouse and/or family and friends would think less of me if I lost my job.   Yes   No
2. Christians ought to prioritize their lives by putting God first, family second, church third, and so on.   Yes   No
3. Someday I'd like to get to the point where I can really spend quality time with God.   Yes   No
4. I've given up trying to solve certain problems in my life. They're just too

big and too complex. I'll just have to live with them.	Yes	No
5. When my spouse asks me questions, I often find myself preoccupied with problems at work.	Yes	No
6. I think I'd probably be more fulfilled if I were in the ministry.	Yes	No
7. The reason most people don't grow as Christians is because they just don't want to badly enough.	Yes	No
8. I've learned that in this life you can't depend on anybody but yourself.	Yes	No
9. I could easily list a dozen ways in which I'm failing as a Christian.	Yes	No
10. The business world is so corrupt that the immorality is bound to rub off on Christians who work in it.	Yes	No
11. I often can't sleep because thoughts about work keep me awake.	Yes	No
12. I believe religion is religion and business is business and, for better or worse, that's the way things are.	Yes	No
13. For a long time I've tolerated habits that I know I should break.	Yes	No
14. Evangelism should be our number-one priority, because only people will last for eternity.	Yes	No
15. I'm trying to work hard and put away a nest egg now so that later on I'll have more time to spend with my family.	Yes	No
16. When it comes to growing in the faith, I believe that you have to "let go and let God."	Yes	No
17. I'm addicted to a certain substance or		

to certain behaviors.   Yes   No

18. I feel that the problem with Christianity is that it just doesn't understand
the way the world operates.   Yes   No

19. I frequently have to miss events and
activities that my children are in
because I have to work or travel.   Yes   No

20. Because I'm not in full-time Christian
ministry, my job doesn't really count as
much to God as a pastor's or a
missionary's.   Yes   No

21. I've set my career goals, and I'm not
about to let anyone or anything prevent
me from achieving them.   Yes   No

22. When I face a problem at work, one of
the last things I do is pray.   Yes   No

23. I'd be a better Christian if only I'd
learn more about the Bible.   Yes   No

24. Someday I hope I'll be able to give my
family the attention they deserve.   Yes   No

25. I feel that God has "put me on the
shelf" because of mistakes in my past.   Yes   No

26. While I'm pretty well organized at
work, I rarely if ever set goals for my
family life.   Yes   No

27. Ministers and missionaries are called to
do God's work, and I'm called to help
pay for it.   Yes   No

28. I have a hard time relaxing. I'd just as
soon be working.   Yes   No

29. If I attended church more, I'd certainly
become a better Christian.   Yes   No

30. I find that work is taking up more and
more of my time and energy.   Yes   No

SCORING

This inventory is not a scientific survey. However your responses may indicate some fundamental misunderstandings or problems you have about your work and how God sees it.

Did you circle Yes for questions 1, 5, 11, 12, 15, 19, 22, 24, 26, 28, and 30? If so, you may be going to work with some very secular attitudes and values. You'll want to carefully read or review Chapter 3.

Did you circle Yes for questions 2, 6, 7, 10, 14, 16, 20, 23, 27, or 29? If so, you may be going to work with some misconceptions about the Bible's teaching on work and Christian growth. You'll want to carefully read or review Chapter 4.

Did you circle Yes for questions 3, 4, 8, 9, 13, 15, 17, 18, 21, 24, or 25? If so, you may be suffering from one or more personal obstacles that can prevent you from balancing time demands. You'll want to carefully read or review Chapter 5.

Suggestion: Ask someone who knows you well, such as your spouse or a close friend, to go through this inventory and give his or her evaluation of how you measure up in each area. Then compare your responses. This is a great way to achieve objectivity and make this exercise more useful.

PART THREE
SUGGESTED TIME: 10 MINUTES

We want you to get the most you can from this book and the sessions that follow. But much depends on you and what you plan to gain from this experience. Reflect for a few moments on how you would complete the statement below, then fill in your response in the space provided.

As a result of going through this book and the exercises in this study guide, I'd like to see changes in my life such as . . .

ON YOUR OWN

1. Memorize Ephesians 5:15-17: "Therefore be careful how you walk not as unwise men, but as wise, making the most of your time, because the days are evil. So then do not be foolish, but understand what the will of the Lord is."

2. Study Luke 14:28-32.
   a. What would you have to change in your life to obtain a balanced lifestyle?

   b. What would you be willing to pay for such balance?

3. Read 1 Timothy 4:7-8. What are the benefits of self-discipline?

4. To prepare for Session 2, carefully read Chapter 6, "The Pentathlon."

Session 2

In this session, you'll look closely at a biblical model for planning called the Pentathlon.

PART ONE

SUGGESTED TIME: 30-35 MINUTES

In Chapter 6, Doug presented the concept of the Pentathlon, the idea that the Bible gives us five major categories of life in which we're to please God. Discuss the following questions:

1. List the five areas of the Pentathlon.

2. How does the Pentathlon concept differ from the traditional hierarchy of God first, family second, church third, and so on?

3. What would it cost you to set limited goals in your job or career so that you could be faithful to God in nonwork areas?

4. Of the five areas of the Pentathlon, which one
   seems to hold the most problems for you? Why?

5. a. How many hours might a person work and still
   be faithful to God in nonwork areas if he or she
   were . . .
   married, with children?
   married, without children?
   a single parent?
   single, without children?
   retired?
   b. Discuss your answers in your group.

PART TWO
SUGGESTED TIME: 25-35 MINUTES

The Pentathlon is simply a way to describe how the Bible
(particularly Paul's letters in the New Testament) addresses the major categories of life. Fill in the chart below
by working your way through one section of Scripture
that illustrates the Pentathlon, Colossians 3:1–4:6. If you
have a group, divide up the passage and work in pairs.
Two examples are given.

Verse(s)	Command or Principle Given	Area of Pentathlon to Which Scripture Applies
3:5	We should not allow evil to have its way in us.	Personal Life
4:1	Employers should be fair to employees.	Work

When you've completed the chart, discuss your findings with the rest of your group. You may want to fill in your own chart more completely after hearing the others' responses.

ON YOUR OWN

1. Review your memorization of Ephesians 5:15-17.
2. Memorize Ephesians 4:15: "But speaking the truth in love we are to grow up in all aspects into Him, who is the head, even Christ."
3. Complete a chart similar to the one in Part Two for Romans 12:1–15:7 and another for Ephesians 4:1–6:20. (Note: This would make an excellent ongoing exercise to work on throughout the next several sessions.)

4. If you are married, discuss the Pentathlon concept with your spouse.
   a. In which area(s) do each of you do best?

   b. Which area(s) do each of you need to work on?

5. In preparation for Session 3, carefully read Chapter 8, "'A-P-P-L-Ying' the Pentathlon," Chapter 9, "Analyze the Scriptures," and Chapter 10, "Take a Personal Inventory."

Session 3

*In this session, you'll learn how to find
principles for godly living from the Bible and
evaluate your own strengths and weaknesses
in applying God's Word.*

PART ONE

SUGGESTED TIME: 35-40 MINUTES

Chapter 8 presents a method for using the Pentathlon as a model for planning your life, called A-P-P-L-Y. The first step in this process is to "Analyze the Scriptures." In the following exercise, you'll consider how to draw practical principles for living from the Bible. This skill will enable you to analyze God's Word on your own in such a way that it makes a difference in your life.

A biblical principle is a basic truth taught by the Bible that applies to life. This truth may be explicitly taught, or it may be implied by the general context of a passage. As you look for biblical principles and formulate them into clear statements, keep the following in mind:

• Valid principles have clear biblical support. You shouldn't have to wrench a verse out of context or read into what a verse clearly says to find a valid principle.

•Valid principles are those that have practical application to life. You should easily be able to point out what a person would do or not do if he lived by a valid principle.

•Valid principles are consistent with the rest of the Bible. If you find yourself contradicting the clear teaching of Scripture, you probably have not found a valid principle.

•Ecclesiastes 5:4: We should follow through on financial commitments made to churches and ministries.

•Romans 13:1: We should obey the government because it is an authority instituted by God.

•James 1:27: We should help those who have financial needs.

(Chapter 9 lists dozens of other scriptural passages that illustrate biblical principles.)

1. List two or three biblical principles of which you're aware, and then describe them to your group. (Include a Bible reference for each, if you know one.)

2. It's easy to spot principles in some passages of Scripture, because they give us direct commands and exhortations. For instance, what are some principles taught by the following passages?

1 John 3:16-18: "We know love by this, that He laid down His life for us; and we ought to lay down our lives for the brethren. But whoever has the world's

goods, and beholds his brother in need and closes his heart against him, how does the love of God abide in him? Little children, let us not love with word or with tongue, but in deed and truth."

Galatians 5:15: "But if you bite and devour one another, take care lest you be consumed by one another."

Hebrews 12:14-15: "Pursue peace with all men, and the sanctification without which no one will see the Lord. See to it that no one comes short of the grace of God; that no root of bitterness springing up causes trouble, and by it many be defiled."

3. Some Bible passages, however, are narrative; they relate stories and parables. Such passages usually imply principles, though they do not state them directly. Read about the incident of Joseph and Potiphar's wife in Genesis 39. Then list four more principles implied in this story, in addition to the example listed.
a. *Success is ultimately something that God causes (verses 2-3).*

b. _____

c. _____

d. _____

e. _____

4. Other Bible passages are poetic in nature, and like narrative only imply principles rather than state them directly. Read Psalm 127 and add two more principles to the example listed.
a. *The ultimate outcome of our labor is dependent on God (verse 1).*

b. _____

c. _____

PART TWO
SUGGESTED TIME: 20-30 MINUTES

If you have not yet completed the personal inventory in Chapter 10, do so now. When you have finished the inventory, review your responses and then do the following exercises.

1. For each area of the Pentathlon, select one way in which you are doing reasonably well and one way in which you could mprove. An example is given.

In my personal life
•*I have a good time of prayer nearly every day.*
•*I have a bad habit of talking about people behind their backs.*

a. In my personal life

b. In my family

c. In my work

d. In my church

e. In my community

2. Depending on how comfortable you feel with your group, share some or all of these observations with the others.

ON YOUR OWN

1. Review your memorization of Ephesians 4:15, 5:15-17.
2. Memorize part or all of Psalm 19:7-11:

> The law of the LORD is perfect, restoring the soul;
> The testimony of the LORD is sure, making wise the simple.
> The precepts of the LORD are right, rejoicing the heart;
> The commandment of the LORD is pure, enlightening the eyes.
> The fear of the LORD is clean, enduring forever;
> The judgments of the LORD are true; they are righteous altogether.
> They are more desirable than gold, yes, than much fine gold;
> Sweeter also than honey and the drippings of the honeycomb.

Moreover, by them Thy servant is warned;
In keeping them there is great reward.

3. Review your responses to Part Two of this session
   with someone who knows you well, such as your
   spouse or a close friend.
4. Find as many principles for godly living as you can
   in each of the following Scripture passages: Genesis
   2:8-9,15; Nehemiah 1:1-11; Psalm 139; Proverbs
   6:16-19; John 15:1-7; Acts 19:8-10; 1 Timothy 4:12;
   Titus 2:9-10; James 4:13-16.

Session 4

In this exercise you'll set goals in each of the five areas of the Pentathlon.

PART ONE

SUGGESTED TIME: 50-60 MINUTES

1. Begin by identifying one way you'd like to grow in each area of the Pentathlon. Don't worry about the wording for now, or even how general your intentions sound. An example is given.

Work: I need to be a more faithful employee on my job.

Personal Life

Family

Work

Church

Community

When you've completed this list, briefly share part of it with your group.

2. Now formulate each of the intentions you listed in terms of a goal. Again, don't worry too much about wording. Just try to attach a practical step that would take you a bit further toward achieving your intention. An example is given.

Work: I'm going to start getting to work on time.

Personal Life

Family

Work

Church

Community

When you've completed this exercise, briefly share part or all of your goals with your group.

3. Now review the goals determined under question 2 above, and revise them into *specific*, *measurable*, and *achievable* steps you can take. Be as precise as you can. An example is given.

Work: When I get up, I'll reset my alarm for 7:30, to remind me that I have to leave for work in five minutes.

Personal Life

Family

Work

Church

Community

Again, share part or all of your revised goals with
your group. Help each other by suggesting ways to
make your goals even more specific, measurable,
achievable, and compatible.

4. If you have a schedule book or calendar with you,
write your goals into your schedule where you'll be
sure and see them.

PART TWO
SUGGESTED TIME: 5-10 MINUTES

Spend some time praying for each person in the group
that God will help him or her to follow through on the
goals and commitments that have been made.

ON YOUR OWN

1. Review your memorization of Ephesians 4:15,
5:15-17, and Psalm 19:7-11.
2. Review the goals that you have developed in this
session with someone who knows you well, such as
your spouse or a close friend.

3. If you haven't already done so, write your goals into your schedule or on your calendar, where you'll be reminded of your commitments.
4. In preparation for Session 5, carefully read Chapter 12, "Make Yourself Liable to Others."

Session 5

*In this session, you'll develop a support system
of people to encourage you in your growth.*

PART ONE
SUGGESTED TIME: 20-25 MINUTES

Read the following statement and then discuss it together as a group.

> "I'm not the kind of person who talks with people
> about my personal life. I mean, I just don't have
> that kind of personality. Besides, whether or not
> I'm praying regularly or spending enough time
> with my spouse is really nobody else's business.
> That's between me and God or me and my spouse.
> Having people check up on me seems awfully
> legalistic!"

1. Do you agree or disagree with this person's attitude
   toward accountability? Why?

2. What potential benefits of accountability might this
   person be overlooking?

3. Read Hebrews 10:24-25. How does this passage counter the view that a person's life and behavior are a private matter between oneself and God?

PART TWO
SUGGESTED TIME: 15-20 MINUTES

Accountability is the willing decision to abide by certain agreed-upon standards, and the voluntary submission of oneself to a review by others in which one's performance is evaluated in light of those standards.

1. In what ways do you agree or disagree with this definition of accountability?

2. Operating with this understanding of accountability, what might be some of the benefits of holding yourself accountable to others?

PART THREE
SUGGESTED TIME: 10-15 MINUTES

We have found that accountability seems to work best when you hold yourself responsible to others who have:

- Similar values and tastes as you do;
- Similar needs, problems, and issues as you do;
- Similar expectations about the nature and value of accountability, and how it should operate;
- Trustworthiness! This is perhaps most important.

Trust and loyalty will ultimately make or break the accountability you establish with others. If you don't trust someone, you'll never hold yourself accountable to him or her.

In light of these criteria, list below the names of some people to whom you might be willing to hold yourself accountable for reaching your goals. (You may already be accountable to some of them.)

_____   _____

_____   _____

_____   _____

_____   _____

You need not share this list with your group. In the next week or two, contact these people individually and discuss the place of accountability in your lives. Ask each one whether he or she would be willing to help you in your progress as a Christian by holding you accountable for growth.

Note: Depending on the persons involved, you may want to form a small group that meets regularly to discuss how the Bible applies to your lives, for prayer, and for mutual encouragement and accountability.

PART FOUR
SUGGESTED TIME: 10 MINUTES

Go back to the goals you developed in Session 4 and next to each goal place the name of someone who will hold you accountable for following through on your commitment. You might also mention a specific way they will do that (for example, with a phone call, a lunch meeting to review progress, etc.).

ON YOUR OWN

1. Review your memorization of Ephesians 4:15, 5:15-17, and Psalm 19:7-11.
2. Memorize Hebrews 10:24-25: "And let us consider how to stimulate one another to love and good deeds, not forsaking our own assembling together, as is the habit of some, but encouraging one another, and all the more, as you see the day drawing near."
3. Discuss the concept of accountability with someone who knows you well, such as your spouse or a close friend. Consider the following questions.
   a. Are you someone who finds it easy or difficult to stay accountable to someone? Why?

   b. What would accountability mean for you? How would it happen? Who would be involved?

   c. Review your list of potential accountability relationships under Part Three. How could each of these persons help you grow as a person?

   Be sure to contact the people you listed.

4. In preparation for Session 6, carefully read Chapter 13, "Use Yardsticks to Measure Your Progress."

Session 6

A checklist you create will help measure your progress, and examine habits you want to cultivate or need to eliminate. You'll also evaluate what you've learned from this book.

PART ONE

SUGGESTED TIME: 10 MINUTES

Set up the checklist on page 216, using the goals you developed in Session 4 (or new ones, if you wish), and use it to track your progress this week. Refer to the example on page 151.

PART TWO

SUGGESTED TIME: 20-25 MINUTES

Despite the explosion of time-management books and seminars, few users of these resources make many long-term changes. Part of the reason is that such materials rarely address the deeper problem of deeply ingrained, longheld habit patterns.

1. Why are habits so difficult to break or establish?

GOALS	SUNDAY	MONDAY	TUESDAY	WEDNESDAY	THURSDAY	FRIDAY	SATURDAY	OKAY
PERSONAL LIFE								
FAMILY								
WORK								
CHURCH								
COMMUNITY								

2. Our Christian growth is largely a matter of "sloughing off" old, fleshly habits and establishing new, God-honoring habits. (See Ephesians 4:22-24. The same idea occurs in Colossians 3.)

a. Name two habit patterns that you need to break.

b. Name two habit patterns that you need to cultivate.

Note: It may help here to review your responses to the personal inventory in Chapter 10.

3. By now, you should be familiar with the A-P-P-L-Y concept. On your own, following this session, use the A-P-P-L-Y concept with each of the four habit patterns you have listed.

Analyze the Scriptures

Personal Inventory

Planned Steps for Action

Liable to Others

Yardstick for Evaluation

PART THREE
SUGGESTED TIME: 15-25 MINUTES

You would be wise to complete the evaluation form on pages 221-222 as a way of analyzing what you've gained from this book and these sessions. Discuss the following questions with your group:

1. What was the best thing about this group experience?

2. What progress have you made toward balancing competing time demands?

3. What one, specific way would you especially like to grow in the coming months?

4. a. Is a discussion group like you've had something you'd like to continue in the future?

   b. If so, what practical issues or topics would be helpful to study together?

PART FOUR
SUGGESTED TIME: 10 MINUTES

Conclude the group session with prayer.

•Thank God for the specific things you've learned and the ways He's already helped you grow.
•Ask God to give each group member strength, courage, and discipline to follow through with the goals and commitments each one has made.

ON YOUR OWN

1. Review your memorization of Ephesians 4:15 and 5:15-17, Psalm 19:7-4, and Hebrews 10:24-25.
2. Use the A-P-P-L-Y concept to finish your work on habits under Part Two (pages 215, 217).
3. If you have not done so, complete the evaluation form on pages 221-222.
4. Evaluate the value of this book and what you've gained from it with someone who knows you well, such as your spouse or a close friend.

Evaluation Form

If you've read this book and worked through all of the exercises in the six sessions in the study guide, you've done a lot of constructive work toward balancing competing time demands. Now complete the job by evaluating your experience.

1. What percentage of the exercises and questions did you complete?

2. If you were part of a discussion group, how many of the group meetings did you participate in?

3. To what extent do you think this experience will make a difference in your life and how did you manage it?

1	2	3	4	5
No Difference				Major Difference

4. Look back at your response to the question asked in Part Three of Session 1 (page 196). You hoped to gain something from this experience. Did you?

5. Describe how this experience could have been more helpful.

WE WANT TO HEAR
FROM YOU!

Bill and I would like to know how this material has affected your life, and how we can improve our resources to be more helpful. Please complete the two statements that follow and send your responses to

Doug Sherman
Career Impact Ministries
P.O. Box 14115
Washington, DC 20044-4115
1-800-4-IMPACT

Include your name and address on the page with your responses.

As a result of your book, *How to Balance Competing Time Demands*, I've changed my life in the following way:

One way this book could have been more helpful to me is: